FOUNDATION 1

G000269575

MASTERING ↗ MATHEMATICS

FOR EDEXCEL GCSE

Practice • Reinforcement • Progress

Assessment Consultant and Editor: **Keith Pledger**

Keith Pledger, Gareth Cole and Joe Petran

Series Editor: Roger Porkess

HODDER
EDUCATION
AN HACHETTE UK COMPANY

The publisher would like to thank the following for permission to reproduce copyright material:

Photo credits

p.16 © scanrail – 123RF; **p.93** © zuzule – Fotolia; **p.94t** © Syda Productions – Fotolia; **p.94b** © Stanislav Halcin – Fotolia; **p.104** © Ingram Publishing – Thinkstock/Getty Images; **p.105** © Lana Langlois – 123RF.

Although every effort has been made to ensure that website addresses are correct at time of going to press, Hodder Education cannot be held responsible for the content of any website mentioned. It is sometimes possible to find a relocated web page by typing in the address of the home page for a website in the URL window of your browser.

Orders: please contact Bookpoint Ltd, 130 Milton Park, Abingdon, Oxon OX14 4SB. Telephone: (44) 01235 827720. Fax: (44) 01235 400454. Lines are open 9.00–17.00, Monday to Saturday, with a 24-hour message answering service. Visit our website at www.hoddereducation.co.uk.

© Keith Pledger, Gareth Cole, Joe Petran 2016

First published in 2016 by

Hodder Education

An Hachette UK Company,

50 Victoria Embankment

London EC4Y 0DZ

Impression number	5	4	3	2	1
Year	2020	2019	2018	2017	2016

Cover photo © agsandrew - Fotolia

Illustrations by Integra

Typeset in India by Integra Software Services Pvt. Ltd., Pondicherry

Printed in Great Britain by CPI Group (UK) Ltd, Croydon CR0 4YY

A catalogue record for this title is available from the British Library.

ISBN 9781471874451

Contents

NUMBER

Strand 1 Calculating

Strand 2 Using our number system

Strand 3 Accuracy

Strand 4 Fractions

Strand 5 Percentages

Strand 6 Ratio and proportion

Contents

ALGEBRA

GEOMETRY AND MEASURES

Strand 6 Three-dimensional shapes

STATISTICS AND PROBABILITY

Strand 1 Statistical measures

Strand 2 Statistical diagrams

Strand 4 Probability

How to get the most from this book

Introduction

This book is part of the Mastering Mathematics for Edexcel GCSE series and supports the textbook by providing lots of extra practice questions for the Foundation tier.

This Practice Book is structured to match the Foundation Student's Book and is likewise organised by key areas of the specification: Number, Algebra, Geometry & Measures and Statistics & Probability. Every chapter in this book accompanies its corresponding chapter from the textbook, with matching titles for ease of use.

Please note: the 'Moving On' units in the Student's Book cover prior knowledge only, so do not have accompanying chapters in this Practice Book. For this reason, although the running order of the Practice Book follows the Student's Book, you may notice that some Strand/Unit numbers appear to be missing, or do not start at '1'.

Progression through each chapter

Chapters include a range of questions that increase in difficulty as you progress through the exercise. There are three levels of difficulty across the Student's Books and Practice Books in this series. These are denoted by shaded spots on the right hand side of each page. Levels broadly reflect GCSE Maths grades as follows:

Low difficulty   GCSE Maths grades 1–3   ●○○

Medium difficulty   GCSE Maths grades 4–6   ●●○

High difficulty   GCSE Maths grades 7–9   ●●●

You might wish to start at the beginning of each chapter and work through so you can see how you are progressing.

Question types

There is also a range of question types included in each chapter, which are denoted by codes to the left hand side of the question or sub-question where they appear. These are examples of the types of question that you will need to practice in readiness for the GCSE Maths Foundation exam.

PS Practising skills

These questions are all about building and mastering the essential techniques that you need to succeed.

DF Developing fluency

These give you practice of using your skills for a variety of purposes and contexts, building your confidence to tackle any type of question.

PB Problem solving

These give practice of using your problem solving skills in order to tackle more demanding problems in the real world, in other subjects and within Maths itself.

Next to any question, including the above question types, you may also see the below code. This means that it is an exam-style question

ES Exam style

This question reflects the language, style and wording of a question that you might see in your GCSE Maths Foundation exam.

Answers

There are answers to every question within the book on our website.

Please visit: www.hoddereducation.co.uk/MasteringmathsforEdexcelGCSE

Number Strand 1 Calculating Unit 7 BIDMAS

PS PRACTISING SKILLS   **DF** DEVELOPING FLUENCY   **PB** PROBLEM SOLVING   **ES** EXAM-STYLE

PS **1** Work these out. ● ○ ○

    a $(8 + 6) \times 3$

    b $8 + 6 \times 3$

    c $8 + (6 \times 3)$

    d $(18 - 6) \div 3$

    e $18 - 6 \div 3$

    f $18 \div (6 - 3)$

PS **2** Work these out. ● ○ ○

    a $17 - 9 \div 3$

    b $(18 - 9) \div 3$

    c $17 - (9 \div 3)$

    d $18 \div 9 - 3$

    e $18 + 9 \div 3$

    f $18 - (9 \div 3)$

DF **3** Find the value of $p^2 + (q + r)^2$ when ● ○ ○

    a $p = 2, q = 3, r = 4$

    b $p = 3, q = 5, r = 7$

    c $p = 10, q = 2, r = 3$

    d $p = 5, q = 2, r = 3$

    e $p = 4, q = 5, r = 6$

    f $p = 10, q = 7, r = 3$

PS **4** Work these out. ● ○ ○

    a $5 \times (2 + 8 \times 3^2)$

    b $(5 \times 2) + (8 \times 3^2)$

    c $5 \times (2 + 8) \times 3^2$

    d $5 \times (8 \div 2 \times 3^2)$

e $(8 \times 2) + (18 \div 3^2)$

f $5 \times (8 \div 2) \times 3^2$

PB **5** Penny takes a taxi which charges £2, plus £1 for every mile travelled. ●○○
The driver charges £15 for a five mile journey. Penny says this is incorrect.
Is she right? Explain your answer.

DF **6** Add brackets ( ) to make each statement correct. ●○○

a $8 \times 7 + 6 \div 2 = 59$

b $8 \times 7 + 6 \div 2 = 52$

c $8 \times 7 + 6 \div 2 = 80$

d $6 \times 7 + 8 \div 2^2 = 44$

e $2^3 \times 2 + 10 \div 2 = 48$

f $3^2 \times 3 + 18 \div 3^2 = 29$

PB **7** A Cash & Carry warehouse sells boxes of kitchen rolls. ●○○
Kitchen rolls cost £10 each for the first 12 boxes,
£7 each for the next 15 boxes,
and £5 for the next 20 boxes,
Barry wants to buy 36 boxes.
How much will he pay?

DF **8** Insert the correct symbols below to make these correct. ●○○

a 3 3 3 3 = 36

b 3 3 3 3 = 10

c 3 3 3 3 = 3

PB
ES **9** An electricity company charges a basic fee of £22. ●○○
The company also charges £3 during the daytime when the heating
is on and £1.50 during the night-time when the heating is on.
An office is heated for 20 days and 10 nights.
How much will the electricity company charge?

PB **10** Some of the numbers below must be written as ●○○
indices to make the sums correct. Which ones?

a $32 + (22 \div 2) = 20$

b $(32 + 32) \div (4 \times 22) = 4$

c $102 + 23 + 33 = 150$

Number Strand 1 Calculating
Unit 8 Multiplying decimals

PS — PRACTISING SKILLS   **DF** — DEVELOPING FLUENCY   **PB** — PROBLEM SOLVING   **ES** — EXAM-STYLE

The questions in this unit should be answered *without* the use of a calculator.

PS 1 Find these.

    a 0.8×0.4

    b 0.7×0.8

    c 0.9×0.7

    d 32×0.04

    e 66×0.66

    f 127×0.005

    g $23 \times 0.6 \times 0.2$

    h $0.04 \times 0.5 \times 0.6$

    i $1250 \times 0.08 \times 0.02$

PS 2 Work out the cost of these.

    a 8 balloons at £1.23 each

    b 7 tickets at £22.75 each

    c 25 bracelets at £26.34 each

    d 12 packets of crisps at £0.55 each

    e 180 roof tiles at £2.42 each

    f 32 plants at £2.45 each

PS 3 You know that $27 \times 59 = 1593$. Use it to find these.

    a 2.7×5.9

    b 27×0.59

    c 270×0.59

    d 0.27×0.59

    e 2.7×0.0059

    f 0.027×0.0059

PB **ES** **4** Charlie and Sam are going to France. Charlie exchanges £198 at an exchange rate of £1 = €1.39. Sam exchanges £212 at an exchange rate of £1 = €1.37.

How many Euros (€) do they have in total?

DF **5** Find these.

a $5 \times (-0.3)$

b $0.5 \times (-0.3)$

c $(-0.5) \times (-0.3)$

d $7 \times (-2.4)$

e $(-2.7) \times (-2.3)$

f $(-127) \times (-0.115)$

DF **6** Gavin fills up his car at three different petrol stations during a week. At the first station he buys 29 litres of petrol at £1.35 per litre. At the second station he buys 27.2 litres of petrol at £1.30 per litre. At the third he buys 31.5 litres of petrol at £1.32 per litre.

How much does he pay in total?

PB **ES** **7** Use of a gym costs £4.45 per hour or £69.50 for a monthly membership. Nicola expects to use the gym for 1.5 hours per day for 9 days of each month.

Should she choose to pay by the hour or take up monthly membership? Show your working.

PB **ES** **8** A monkey sanctuary houses 35 monkeys. Each monkey costs £5.34 per day to feed, over 365 days of the year. The entry fee for the monkey sanctuary is £5.50. The sanctuary has 21 000 visitors per year.

Does the monkey sanctuary make enough money to feed the monkeys? You may use a calculator for this question.

PB **ES** **9** A window cleaner has to clean 130 windows in a tower block. Each window measures 50 cm by 70 cm. Cleaning fluid costs £1.58 to clean every 10 m^2.

How much will it cost the window cleaner to clean the 130 windows?

Number Strand 1 Calculating
Unit 9 Dividing decimals

PS – PRACTISING SKILLS **DF** – DEVELOPING FLUENCY **PB** – PROBLEM SOLVING **ES** – EXAM-STYLE

PS **1** Work out these.

a $2.18 \div 2$

b $13.8 \div 3$

c $21 \div 4$

d $38 \div 8$

e $66 \div 5$

f $0.072 \div 6$

g $23.125 \div 5$

h $62 \div 8$

i $39.168 \div 9$

PS **2** Work out the cost of one item in each of these.

a 8 bottles of milk cost £6.24

b 11 theatre tickets cost £313.50

c 25 DVDs cost £246.25

d 19 packets of peanuts cost £13.68

e 180 light bulbs cost £277.20

f 6 cars cost £53 970

PS **3** You know that $35 \div 5 = 7$. Use it to find these.

a $3.5 \div 5$

b $3.5 \div 0.5$

c $350 \div 0.5$

d $0.35 \div 5$

e $3.5 \div 0.05$

f $0.035 \div 0.005$

DF **4** Work out these.

  a $78 \div (-3)$

  b $(-61) \div 5$

  c $(-5.7) \div 3$

  d $2 \times 7 \div (-2.8)$

  e $54 \div (-2.7) \times (-2.3)$

  f $(-12) \times (-8.1) \div 3$

DF **5** Four people split a restaurant bill of £176.68 equally.
How much does each person pay?

DF **6** Mark buys some cheese which costs £2.56 per kilo. He pays £9.60.
How much cheese does he buy?

PB **7** Work out these.

ES

  a In one week, Susan earned £279.50 for working 32.5 hours. Work out Susan's hourly rate of pay.

  b In the same week, Ralph earned £315 for working 37.5 hours. Work out Ralph's hourly rate of pay.

PB **8** In 2014, 12 people hire a coach at a cost of £319.80. Each pay

ES an equal share. In 2015, they hire the same coach which now costs £337.20.
How much extra does each person pay in 2015?

PB **9** Mary bought a car for £9000. She paid a deposit of £1500 and

ES the rest in 24 equal payments.
How much was each repayment?

PB **10** Kayleigh exchanges money in a bank for a holiday and receives

ES €310.08 for £228. Peter exchanges money in a post office and receives €369.84 for £268.
Who gets the best deal?

Number Strand 2 Using our number system Unit 5 Using the number system effectively

 PS PRACTISING SKILLS   **DF** DEVELOPING FLUENCY   **PB** PROBLEM SOLVING   **ES** EXAM-STYLE

PS 1 Work these out. ●○○

   a 8400×1000

   b 8400×100

   c 8400×10

   d 8400×0.1

   e 8400×0.01

   f 8400×0.001

   g 4978×1000

   h 4978×100

   i 4978×10

   j 4978×0.1

   k 4978×0.01

   l 4978×0.001

PS 2 Work these out. ●○○

   a 60×0.1

   b 340×0.1

   c 5400×0.01

   d 2230×0.01

   e 690×0.001

   f 223×0.001

PS **3** Work these out.

    a 2.1×0.1

    b 6.25×0.1

    c 13.7×0.01

    d 245.6×0.01

    e 0.3×0.001

    f 4.57×0.001

PS **4** Work these out.

    a $2.1 \div 0.1$

    b $6.25 \div 0.1$

    c $13.7 \div 0.01$

    d $245.6 \div 0.01$

    e $0.3 \div 0.001$

    f $4.57 \div 0.001$

DF **5** Write the answers to these calculations in order of size, smallest first.

    a 4.8×0.1

    b $3.56 \div 0.1$

    c 29.8×0.01

    d $75.5 \div 0.01$

    e 19.9×0.001

    f $0.72 \div 0.001$

DF **6** Find the missing numbers.

    a $250 \times \square = 25$

    b $250 \div \square = 25$

    c $1.98 \times \square = 1980$

    d $1.98 \div \square = 1980$

    e $654 \times \square = 6.54$

    f $654 \div \square = 6.54$

PB **7** A game of mathematical 'snap' uses cards as shown below.
Use arrows to show which two cards are equal.

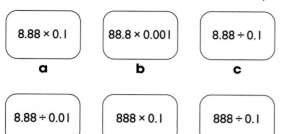

| 8.88 × 0.1 | 88.8 × 0.001 | 8.88 ÷ 0.1 |
| a | b | c |

| 8.88 ÷ 0.01 | 888 × 0.1 | 888 ÷ 0.1 |
| d | e | f |

PB **8** The signpost in Mathsland offers you four routes to your destination.
Which is the shortest?

← 12.7 ÷ 0.01 km

12 700 × 0.1 km →

↑ 127 × 1 km

1.27 ÷ 0.001 km ↓

PB **9** Here are some calculations involving numbers.

| 2.56 × 100 | 2.56 ÷ 100 | 2.56 × 0.1 |

| 2.56 ÷ 0.001 | 2.56 × 0.001 | 2.56 ÷ 0.1 |

Arrange them in order of size from largest to smallest.

Number Strand 2 Using our number system Unit 6 Understanding standard form

PS — PRACTISING SKILLS   DF — DEVELOPING FLUENCY   PB — PROBLEM SOLVING   ES — EXAM-STYLE

PS 1 Write these numbers in standard form.

   a 847

   b 84 700

   c 0.000 847

   d 0.000 000 847

PS 2 Write these numbers in standard form.

   a 620

   b 820 000

   c 20 million

   d 1 millionth

PS 3 Write these as ordinary numbers.

   a 8.52×10^2

   b 3.4×10^{-3}

   c 2.02×10^5

   d 5.762×10^8

   e 4.55×10^{-7}

PS 4 Write these numbers in standard form.

   a 0.003 45

   b 0.000 005 48

   c 0.000 765 4

   d 0.000 000 234 5

DF **5** Write these numbers in standard form.

    a Eight thousand

    b Four fifths

    c Six hundredths

DF **6** Write these quantities in standard form.

    a The distance between the Earth and the Sun is 93 million miles.

    b The area of one person's skin is about 15000 cm².

    c The distance from the equator to the north pole is 20000 km.

    d There are about 400 million stars in the Milky Way.

    e The area of the UK is 243610 km².

DF **7** Write these numbers in order, starting with the smallest.

    a 4.2×10^{-3}

    b 7.21×10^{-2}

    c 0.09

    d 8.2×10^{-3}

    e 5.7×10^{2}

    f 3.6×10^{3}

    g 6.2×10^{2}

    h 0.57

PB **8** The table shows the distances of the Sun to nearby stars.

An astronomer is researching the stars and needs to make sure his list is in order, with the stars nearest to the Sun first. Show the list he needs to write.

Star	Distance from the Sun (in km)
Procyon B	1.08×10^{14}
Barnard's Star	5.67×10^{13}
Proxima Centauri	3.97×10^{13}
Sirius A	8.136×10^{13}
Ross 128	1.031×10^{14}
Wolf 359	7.285×10^{13}
Rigil Kentaurus	4.07×10^{13}
Luyten 726	7.95×10^{13}

Number Strand 3 Accuracy Unit 4 Rounding to 2 decimal places

PS PRACTISING SKILLS   **DF** DEVELOPING FLUENCY   **PB** PROBLEM SOLVING   **ES** EXAM-STYLE

The questions in this unit should be answered *without* the use of a calculator, unless otherwise specified.

PS **1** Round each of these numbers to two decimal places.

    a 2.756

    b 12.462

    c 0.064

    d 0.896

    e 1.997

    f 65.507

    g 0.005

    h 9.995

    i 12.352

    j 10.002

PB **2** Ben buys a packet of seven identical pens for £1.99.
Work out the cost of one pen. Give your answer to the nearest penny.

PB **3** You may use a calculator for this question
Sylvia buys 35.6 litres of petrol at 123.9 pence per litre.
Work out the total cost of the petrol Sylvia bought.
Give your answer in pounds to the nearest penny.

DF **4** Work out the number which is halfway between

    a 2.5 and 5.2

    b 0.23 and 0.24

    c 3.5 and 3.65

    d 2.05 and 2.049

    e 3.2 and 2.3

    f 6.25 and 6.255

g 10 and 10.001

h 7.98 and 8.003

DF ES **5** Here is a rectangle.

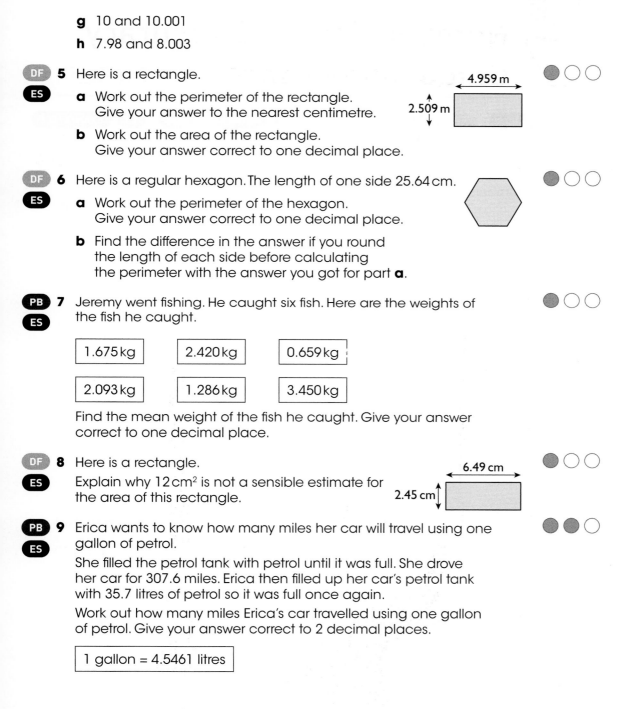

a Work out the perimeter of the rectangle.
Give your answer to the nearest centimetre.

b Work out the area of the rectangle.
Give your answer correct to one decimal place.

4.959 m

2.509 m

DF ES **6** Here is a regular hexagon. The length of one side 25.64 cm.

a Work out the perimeter of the hexagon.
Give your answer correct to one decimal place.

b Find the difference in the answer if you round
the length of each side before calculating
the perimeter with the answer you got for part **a**.

PB ES **7** Jeremy went fishing. He caught six fish. Here are the weights of
the fish he caught.

| 1.675 kg | 2.420 kg | 0.659 kg |

| 2.093 kg | 1.286 kg | 3.450 kg |

Find the mean weight of the fish he caught. Give your answer
correct to one decimal place.

DF ES **8** Here is a rectangle.

Explain why 12 cm² is not a sensible estimate for
the area of this rectangle.

6.49 cm

2.45 cm

PB ES **9** Erica wants to know how many miles her car will travel using one
gallon of petrol.

She filled the petrol tank with petrol until it was full. She drove
her car for 307.6 miles. Erica then filled up her car's petrol tank
with 35.7 litres of petrol so it was full once again.

Work out how many miles Erica's car travelled using one gallon
of petrol. Give your answer correct to 2 decimal places.

| 1 gallon = 4.5461 litres |

13

Number Strand 3 Accuracy
Unit 5 Significance

PS — PRACTISING SKILLS   DF — DEVELOPING FLUENCY   PB — PROBLEM SOLVING   ES — EXAM-STYLE

PS 1 Write down the number of significant figures there are in each of these numbers.

   a 2.75

   b 507

   c 0.0045

   d 1009

   e 0.0306

   f 1.0

PS 2 Write these numbers to two significant figures.

   a 2.75

   b 507

   c 0.00453

   d 1009

   e 0.0306

   f 1.02

PS 3 Write the number 2367450 correct to

   a three significant figures

   b one significant figure

   c two significant figures.

PS 4 Write the number 0.39999 correct to

   a three significant figures

   b one significant figure

   c two significant figures.

PB **5** 17 845 people attended an outdoor concert in a park.

    a The local newspaper gave the attendance to three significant figures. Write the attendance to three significant figures.

    b The local Radio station gave the attendance to two significant figures. Write the attendance to two significant figures.

    c The local TV reporter gave the attendance to one significant figure. Write the attendance to one significant figure.

PB **6** The formula for working out the area of an ellipse is πab.

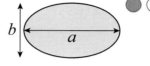

    a Using the value of π as 3.141 59, find the area of the ellipse where $a = 4.50$ and $b = 2.76$. Give the answer correct to three significant figures.

    b Find the difference in the answer to part **a** and the answer if the value of π being used was written to three significant figures. Give the answer correct to three significant figures.

PB **7** Here is part of Gerri's gas bill. It shows the units she used during March.

Work out Gerri's gas bill for March. Give your answer correct to two significant figures.

Gas 2U	
Mrs G Hall 2 High St	April 4th
End of March reading	4593
End of February reading	3976
Units used	617
Cost per unit	15.6 pence
Monthly charge	£10.50

PB **ES** **8** The Earth is 92 955 807 miles away from the Sun. The speed of light is 186 000 miles per second correct to 3 significant figures.

Find the number of seconds it takes for a ray of light to leave the Sun and reach the Earth. Give your answer correct to two significant figures.

DF **ES** **9** The area of a square is 8 cm².

Find the length of one side of the square. Give your answer correct to three siginificant figures.

8 cm²

DF **ES** **10** The volume of a cube is 10 cm³.

Find the length of one side of the cube. Give your answer correct to three significant figures.

10 cm³

PS **ES** **11** Paula ran 10.55 miles in 1 hour 54 minutes.

Work out her average speed in miles per hour. Give your answer correct to two significant figures.

Number Strand 3 Accuracy
Unit 6 Approximation

PS – PRACTISING SKILLS   DF – DEVELOPING FLUENCY   PB – PROBLEM SOLVING   ES – EXAM-STYLE

PS 1 Work out an estimate for the answers to these calculations.

    a 8.87 + 98.35 – 5.08

    b 6.9 × 9.2

    c 210.7 ÷ 6.89

    d 18.9^2

    e $\sqrt{99.54}$

    f $\dfrac{29.7 \times 81.5}{0.529}$

PS 2 A packet of batteries costs £1.95.

Which of these amounts gives a sensible estimate for the cost of five packets of these batteries?

| **A** 40p | **B** £2 | **C** £5 | **D** £10 | **E** £20 |

PS 3 Lucy bought eight mugs for £15.95.

Which one of these amounts gives a sensible estimate for the cost of each mug?

| **A** 20p | **B** £2 | **C** £16 | **D** £120 | **E** £200 |

PB ES 4 John sees some shirts and some jeans for sale in a shop. The shirts are selling at £6.95 each and jeans are selling at £14.99 each. John has £50 to spend. He wants to buy three shirts and two pairs of jeans.

Estimate if he has enough money. Give reasons for your answer.

DF ES 5 Rob saves £42 a week for a year.

Estimate the amount he saves in a year.

DF ES 6 Robina pays £6.85 a month for her mobile phone call plan.

Approximately how much does she have to pay for a year?

PB
ES
7 Here is part of Harry's electricity bill. It shows the units he used during May.

Harry has saved £65 to pay this bill. Estimate if he has saved enough. Explain your answer.

Electricity 4us	
Mr H Styles 12 Lower Rd	June 4th
End of May reading	5396
End of April reading	4979
Units used	417
Cost per unit	9.5 pence
Monthly charge	£19.50

DF **8** Becky drove a distance of 295 miles in 5 hours 14 minutes.
Make an estimate of her average speed in miles per hour.

DF **9** Liam saves 5% of his pay each month for five years. His average monthly pay is £1025.
Estimate how much money Liam has saved in the 5 years.

DF **10** It takes Rachel two hours 10 minutes a day to travel to and from work. She works 5 days a week for 48 weeks a year.
Estimate how many hours Rachel spends travelling in a year.

PB **11** Rodney buys items at car boot sales and sells them on an internet website. Here are the items he bought and sold last week.
Find an approximation for Rodney's total profit last week.

Item	Bought for	Sold for
Doll	£9.99	£21.65
Jigsaw	£5.05	£2.95
Camera	£15.75	£39.85
Computer game	£4.99	£21.06
China ornament	£5.00	£99.99

PB
ES
12 Airi owns a factory that makes plastic toys. The factory makes 395 toys an hour. 10% of the toys are not perfect. The perfect toys are put into bags. The bags are then packed into cartons. Each carton holds 48 bags. The factory makes toys for 8 hours 5 minutes each day.
Estimate the number of cartons that are needed each day.
You must show all your working.

17

Number Strand 4 Fractions
Unit 3 Multiplying fractions

PS — PRACTISING SKILLS   DF — DEVELOPING FLUENCY   PB — PROBLEM SOLVING   ES — EXAM-STYLE

PS **1** Work out these. ●○○

a $\dfrac{1}{2} \times \dfrac{1}{5}$

b $\dfrac{1}{3} \times \dfrac{1}{7}$

c $\dfrac{1}{2} \times \dfrac{3}{4}$

d $\dfrac{1}{3} \times \dfrac{2}{5}$

e $\dfrac{2}{3} \times \dfrac{4}{9}$

f $\dfrac{3}{4} \times \dfrac{2}{7}$

g $\dfrac{3}{4} \times \dfrac{3}{4}$

h $\dfrac{5}{7} \times \dfrac{8}{9}$

PS **2** Work out these. Cancel the fractions before multiplying. ●○○

a $\dfrac{1}{2} \times \dfrac{2}{3}$

b $\dfrac{1}{4} \times \dfrac{8}{9}$

c $\dfrac{1}{5} \times \dfrac{15}{16}$

d $\dfrac{2}{3} \times \dfrac{6}{7}$

e $\dfrac{3}{5} \times \dfrac{5}{8}$

f $\dfrac{3}{4} \times \dfrac{4}{9}$

g $\dfrac{5}{4} \times \dfrac{8}{15}$

h $\dfrac{3}{7} \times \dfrac{14}{33}$

PS **3** Work out these. Cancel the fractions before multiplying. ● ○ ○

   a $\dfrac{1}{3} \times \dfrac{3}{5} \times \dfrac{5}{7}$

   b $\dfrac{2}{5} \times \dfrac{6}{7} \times \dfrac{5}{6}$

   c $\dfrac{4}{7} \times \dfrac{7}{8} \times \dfrac{3}{5}$

   d $\dfrac{4}{9} \times \dfrac{5}{8} \times \dfrac{18}{25}$

   e $\dfrac{9}{14} \times \dfrac{21}{25} \times \dfrac{5}{6}$

   f $\dfrac{27}{72} \times \dfrac{64}{81} \times \dfrac{15}{16}$

DF **4** Match these cards. ● ○ ○

half of $\frac{3}{8}$	$\frac{3}{8} \times \frac{2}{5}$	$\frac{3}{8}$ of $\frac{3}{4}$	$\frac{3}{4}$ of three quarters
a	**b**	**c**	**d**
$\frac{3}{4} \times \frac{2}{5}$	$\frac{1}{2} \times \frac{3}{8}$	$\frac{3}{8}$ of two fifths	$\frac{3}{4} \times \frac{3}{4}$
e	**f**	**g**	**h**
half of three quarters	three eighths of three quarters	$\frac{1}{2} \times \frac{3}{4}$	three quarters of $\frac{2}{5}$
i	**j**	**k**	**l**

DF **5** Complete these. Which symbol, <, > or = goes in each box? ● ○ ○

   a $\dfrac{4}{5} \times \dfrac{5}{7} \ \square \ \dfrac{4}{7}$

   b $\dfrac{3}{5} \times \dfrac{5}{9} \ \square \ \dfrac{2}{3}$

   c $\dfrac{2}{3} \times \dfrac{3}{4} \ \square \ \dfrac{1}{4}$

   d $\dfrac{4}{7} \times \dfrac{7}{9} \ \square \ \dfrac{5}{9}$

   e $\dfrac{15}{32} \times \dfrac{8}{25} \ \square \ \dfrac{3}{20}$

   f $\dfrac{3}{4} \times \dfrac{8}{9} \ \square \ \dfrac{7}{8} \times \dfrac{4}{7}$

DF **6** Wilber has a stamp collection. He gives $\frac{3}{7}$ of his stamp collection to Percy. Percy throws $\frac{1}{6}$ of these stamps away.

What fraction of Wilber's stamp collection did Percy throw away?

PB **7** Oliver gets an energy bill each year. Last year, $\frac{7}{12}$ of Oliver's energy bill was for electricity. Oliver heats his water using electricity. $\frac{4}{5}$ of this electricity was for heating water.

What fraction of Oliver's energy bill was for heating water?

DF **8** Complete these. What fraction goes in each box?

a $\frac{3}{7} \times \square = \frac{6}{35}$

b $\square \times \frac{2}{3} = \frac{8}{15}$

c $\frac{4}{5} \square = \frac{28}{45}$

d $\square \times \frac{5}{6} = \frac{5}{8}$

e $\frac{9}{10} \times \square = \frac{9}{14}$

f $\frac{3}{8} \times \square = \frac{1}{12}$

DF **9** Lynne cuts a piece of paper, A, into two parts, B and C. She then cuts part C into two parts, D and E.

Part C is $\frac{1}{3}$ of part A. Part D is $\frac{3}{10}$ of part C.

What fraction of part A is

a part B

b part D

c part E?

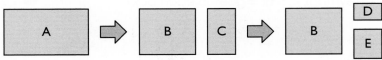

PB **ES** **10** Zebedee is given some money for his birthday. He spends $\frac{1}{4}$ of it on music and $\frac{2}{3}$ of what is left on a pair of trousers.

What fraction of his birthday money did Zebedee spend on trousers?

PB **ES** **11** At a pantomime, $\frac{5}{9}$ of the audience are children the rest are adults. $\frac{3}{5}$ of the children are boys. $\frac{2}{3}$ of the adults are females. What fraction of the audience are

  a boys

  b adult males?

PB **ES** **12** Jake bought a car. At the end of the first year the value of the car was $\frac{3}{4}$ of its value at the beginning of the year. At the end of each following year, the value of the car was $\frac{8}{9}$ of its value at the beginning of that year.

  Work out the smallest number of years for the car to more than halve its initial value.

DF **13** Work out the area of each of these shapes. Give your answers as fractions in their simplest form.

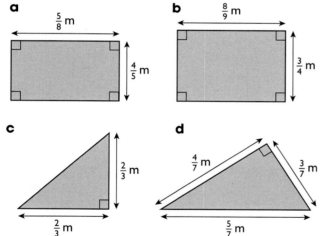

a $\frac{5}{8}$ m, $\frac{4}{5}$ m

b $\frac{8}{9}$ m, $\frac{3}{4}$ m

c $\frac{2}{3}$ m, $\frac{2}{3}$ m

d $\frac{4}{7}$ m, $\frac{3}{7}$ m, $\frac{5}{7}$ m

Number Strand 4 Fractions Unit 4 Adding and subtracting fractions

PS PRACTISING SKILLS **DF** DEVELOPING FLUENCY **PB** PROBLEM SOLVING **ES** EXAM-STYLE

PS **1** Work out these.

a $\frac{1}{5} + \frac{2}{5}$

b $\frac{4}{7} + \frac{2}{7}$

c $\frac{5}{9} - \frac{3}{9}$

d $\frac{13}{15} - \frac{2}{15}$

e $\frac{3}{20} + \frac{7}{20} + \frac{9}{20}$

f $\frac{5}{17} + \frac{8}{17} - \frac{3}{17}$

g $\frac{10}{13} - \frac{8}{13} + \frac{3}{13}$

h $\frac{9}{11} - \frac{3}{11} - \frac{5}{11}$

PS **2** Work out these.

a $1 - \frac{1}{6}$

b $1 - \frac{2}{7}$

c $1 - \frac{5}{8}$

d $1 - \frac{31}{100}$

e $1 - \frac{1}{10} - \frac{2}{10}$

f $1 - \frac{4}{11} - \frac{2}{11}$

g $1 - \frac{17}{21} + \frac{9}{21}$

h $1 - \frac{27}{35} + \frac{11}{35}$

PS **3** Work out these. Give your answers as fractions in their simplest form. ●○○

   a $\dfrac{1}{8} + \dfrac{1}{4}$

   b $\dfrac{3}{10} + \dfrac{1}{2}$

   c $\dfrac{2}{3} + \dfrac{1}{9}$

   d $\dfrac{3}{4} + \dfrac{1}{12}$

   e $\dfrac{15}{16} - \dfrac{3}{4}$

   f $\dfrac{4}{5} - \dfrac{7}{20}$

   g $\dfrac{13}{18} - \dfrac{4}{9}$

   h $\dfrac{7}{9} - \dfrac{4}{27}$

PS **4** Work out these. Give your answers as fractions in their simplest form. ●○○

   a $\dfrac{1}{3} + \dfrac{1}{4}$

   b $\dfrac{1}{4} + \dfrac{2}{7}$

   c $\dfrac{3}{5} - \dfrac{1}{3}$

   d $\dfrac{5}{7} - \dfrac{2}{3}$

   e $\dfrac{3}{8} + \dfrac{2}{5}$

   f $\dfrac{5}{6} - \dfrac{4}{7}$

   g $\dfrac{3}{8} + \dfrac{5}{12}$

   h $\dfrac{7}{9} - \dfrac{5}{12}$

DF **5** A bag contains only red, yellow and green counters. $\dfrac{2}{9}$ of the counters ●○○
are red. $\dfrac{3}{5}$ of the counters are yellow.

What fraction of the counters are

   a not red

   b red or yellow

   c green?

DF **6** $x = \dfrac{3}{5}, y = \dfrac{1}{7}$. Work out

    a $x + y$

    b $x - y$

    c $2x - 3y$.

DF **7** Complete these. What fraction goes in each box for the answer to be correct?

    a $\dfrac{3}{7} + \square = \dfrac{5}{7}$

    b $\dfrac{56}{99} - \square = \dfrac{27}{99}$

    c $\dfrac{7}{8} - \square = \dfrac{2}{5}$

    d $\dfrac{5}{16} + \square = \dfrac{7}{8}$

    e $\dfrac{5}{9} + \square = \dfrac{2}{3}$

    f $\dfrac{3}{8} + \square = \dfrac{7}{12}$

    g $\dfrac{4}{9} - \square = \dfrac{5}{12}$

    h $\dfrac{19}{27} - \square = \dfrac{7}{18}$

DF **8** Pierre is reading a book. He reads $\dfrac{1}{5}$ of the book on Friday, $\dfrac{1}{4}$ of the book on Saturday and $\dfrac{1}{3}$ of the book on Sunday.

What fraction of the book has he read all together?

DF **9** Work out these. Give your answers as fractions in their simplest form.

    a $1 - \left(\dfrac{5}{8} - \dfrac{2}{5} \right)$

    b $\left(\dfrac{5}{6} + \dfrac{1}{3} \right) - \left(\dfrac{5}{6} - \dfrac{1}{2} \right)$

    c $\left(\dfrac{3}{8} - \dfrac{1}{4} \right) + \left(\dfrac{4}{5} - \dfrac{3}{10} \right)$

PB **ES** **10** The pie chart shows information about the different types of pizza some students like the best. $\dfrac{4}{11}$ of the students like ham and pineapple the best.

    a What fraction of the students like pepperoni the best?

    b What fraction of the students like cheese and tomato the best?

PB
ES
11 Here are three paint pots, pot A, pot B and pot C. All three pots are the same size.

Pot A contains $\frac{1}{5}$ of a pot of paint. Pot B contains twice as much paint as pot A. Pot C contains $\frac{1}{4}$ of a pot of paint.

Jim wants to combine all the paint into one pot. Can he do it? Show how you get your answer.

DF
ES
12 The diagram shows a rectangle.
Work out the perimeter of the rectangle.
Give your answer as a fraction in its simplest form.

$\frac{2}{5}$ m

$\frac{1}{12}$ m

PB
ES
13 Gerard mixes lime cordial with water to make a glass of lime drink.

He uses $\frac{1}{20}$ of a bottle of lime cordial to make each glass of lime drink.
Gerard has $\frac{5}{8}$ of a bottle of lime cordial. He wants to make as many glasses of lime drink as possible.

a How many glasses of the lime drink can he make?

b How much lime cordial does he have left?

PB
ES
14 The volume of a piece of cheese is V cm³. Sarah cuts the piece of cheese into three parts. The volume of the smallest part is $\frac{1}{9}V$ cm³.
The volume of the largest is $\frac{3}{4}V$ cm³.

What is the volume of the remaining part? Give your answer in terms of V.

Number Strand 4 Fractions Unit 5 Working with mixed numbers

PS — PRACTISING SKILLS DF — DEVELOPING FLUENCY PB — PROBLEM SOLVING ES — EXAM-STYLE

PS 1 Copy and complete the table. Change between mixed numbers and top-heavy fractions. The first one has been done for you.

	a	b	c	d	e	f	g	h
Mixed number	$1\frac{3}{5}$	$2\frac{2}{3}$			$3\frac{4}{7}$	$7\frac{5}{6}$		$5\frac{7}{19}$
Top-heavy fraction	$\frac{8}{5}$		$\frac{13}{4}$	$\frac{39}{5}$			$\frac{131}{9}$	

PS 2 Work out these. Write each answer as a mixed number.

a $2\frac{2}{5} + \frac{4}{5}$

b $3\frac{4}{5} - 1\frac{1}{5}$

c $5\frac{5}{7} + 2\frac{4}{7}$

d $3\frac{2}{7} - 1\frac{3}{7}$

e $1\frac{3}{10} + 2\frac{2}{5}$

f $4\frac{1}{3} - 2\frac{2}{9}$

g $2\frac{5}{6} + 3\frac{7}{12}$

h $4\frac{2}{11} - 1\frac{9}{22}$

i $3\frac{7}{15} + 1\frac{13}{20}$

PS **3** Work out these. Write each answer as a mixed number.

    a $1\frac{2}{3} + 1\frac{3}{4}$

    b $3\frac{4}{5} - 1\frac{2}{3}$

    c $4\frac{1}{4} - 2\frac{4}{5}$

    d $3\frac{2}{5} + 1\frac{1}{6}$

    e $1\frac{5}{6} + 2\frac{2}{7}$

    f $3\frac{2}{9} + 2\frac{3}{5}$

    g $3\frac{5}{7} - 1\frac{7}{9}$

    h $5\frac{5}{12} - 2\frac{6}{15}$

    i $3\frac{4}{15} + 5\frac{7}{45}$

PS **4** Work out these. Cancel the fractions before multiplying.

    a $2\frac{2}{3} \times \frac{3}{4}$

    b $\frac{3}{5} \times 3\frac{3}{4}$

    c $1\frac{3}{5} \times 3\frac{1}{3}$

    d $3\frac{1}{5} \times 1\frac{3}{4}$

    e $1\frac{1}{5} \times 4\frac{1}{6}$

    f $5\frac{1}{4} \times 2\frac{2}{7}$

    g $3\frac{3}{5} \times \frac{8}{9}$

    h $2\frac{2}{7} \times 4\frac{3}{8}$

    i $4\frac{4}{9} \times 5\frac{5}{8}$

DF **5** Kerry has two oil drums, P and Q. P contains $5\frac{3}{4}$ gallons of oil.
Q contains $3\frac{2}{5}$ gallons of oil.

    a Work out the total amount of oil in the two oil drums.

    b P contains more oil than Q. How much more?

DF **6** Giles plays draughts. He can win, lose or draw each game he plays.
Last year, Giles won $55\frac{3}{4}$% of his games and he lost $32\frac{5}{6}$% of his games.
What percentage of his games did he draw?

DF **7** Here are two rectangles. Work out

    a the area

    b the perimeter of each rectangle. Give your answers as mixed
    numbers in their simplest form.

DF **8** In the triangle ABC, angle ABC = $61\frac{2}{5}°$ and angle BCA = $72\frac{2}{3}°$.
Work out the size of angle CAB.

PB
ES **9** Riley uses a lorry to take gravel to a building site. The table gives
information about the amount of gravel Riley took to the building
site each day last week.

Riley says: 'I took more than $12\frac{1}{2}$ tons of gravel to the building site
last week.' Is he right? Show how you get your answer.

Day	Monday	Tuesday	Wednesday	Thursday	Friday
Amount of gravel (in tons)	$2\frac{3}{4}$	2	$3\frac{1}{3}$	$1\frac{3}{5}$	3

PB
ES **10** Liam drives a car in California. On Saturday, he drove his car to see
his sister. He used $\frac{2}{3}$ of a tank of petrol. On Sunday, Liam refilled
the tank and drove his car to see his brother. He used $\frac{5}{6}$ of a tank
of petrol. The petrol tank in Liam's car holds $7\frac{3}{5}$ gallons of petrol.
He pays $2.80 for a gallon of petrol.
How much did Liam pay in total for the petrol he used to see
his sister and brother?

PB **11** Here are two signposts on a footpath.

Work out the distance on the footpath between

a Stoneford and Upton

b the two sign posts

c Upton and Pen Hill.

PB
ES **12** The diagram shows an empty room. The room is in the shape of a cuboid. An extractor fan is used to filter the air in the room. It takes the extractor fan 3 minutes 20 seconds to filter $2\,m^3$ of air.

Work out the shortest time it takes the extractor fan to filter all the air in the room.

DF **13** $A = 2\frac{4}{5}$, $B = 3\frac{4}{7}$. Work out

a $A + B$

b AB

c $5A + 7B$

d $5(B - A)$

Number Strand 4 Fractions
Unit 6 Dividing fractions

PS — **PRACTISING SKILLS**   **DF** — **DEVELOPING FLUENCY**   **PB** — **PROBLEM SOLVING**   **ES** — **EXAM-STYLE**

The questions in this unit should be answered *without* the use of a calculator.

PS **1** Pair each number with its reciprocal.

$\frac{1}{2}$	5	$\frac{3}{10}$	$\frac{2}{5}$	$3\frac{1}{3}$

$\frac{4}{15}$	2	$2\frac{1}{2}$	$\frac{1}{5}$	$3\frac{3}{4}$

PS **2** Change each of these into a multiplication and then work out the answer.

    a $5 \div \frac{1}{2}$

    b $8 \div \frac{1}{3}$

    c $9 \div \frac{1}{4}$

    d $10 \div \frac{2}{3}$

    e $15 \div \frac{3}{5}$

    f $20 \div \frac{5}{7}$

    g $\frac{3}{5} \div 4$

    h $\frac{2}{3} \div 5$

    i $\frac{4}{7} \div 8$

PS **3** Change each of these into a multiplication and then work out the answer. Cancel the fractions before multiplying.

a $\dfrac{7}{10} \div \dfrac{1}{5}$

b $\dfrac{3}{8} \div \dfrac{1}{4}$

c $\dfrac{5}{9} \div \dfrac{1}{3}$

d $\dfrac{9}{16} \div \dfrac{3}{4}$

e $\dfrac{9}{40} \div \dfrac{3}{5}$

f $\dfrac{8}{15} \div \dfrac{4}{5}$

g $\dfrac{5}{9} \div \dfrac{1}{6}$

h $\dfrac{7}{10} \div \dfrac{14}{15}$

i $\dfrac{15}{24} \div \dfrac{9}{16}$

PS **4** Change each of these into a multiplication and then work out the answer. Cancel the fractions before multiplying.

a $2\dfrac{1}{7} \div \dfrac{1}{7}$

b $5\dfrac{2}{3} \div \dfrac{1}{6}$

c $1\dfrac{5}{8} \div \dfrac{1}{4}$

d $\dfrac{3}{4} \div 1\dfrac{1}{8}$

e $\dfrac{8}{15} \div 1\dfrac{1}{5}$

f $\dfrac{5}{12} \div 2\dfrac{2}{9}$

g $3\dfrac{1}{9} \div 1\dfrac{1}{6}$

h $4\dfrac{9}{10} \div 1\dfrac{2}{5}$

i $7\dfrac{4}{7} \div 2\dfrac{2}{21}$

DF **5** A bag contains $1\dfrac{3}{5}$ lbs of sugar. A teaspoon holds $\dfrac{1}{150}$ lbs of sugar.

How many teaspoons of sugar are there in the bag?

DF **6** Which symbol, =, < or > goes in each box?

a $1\frac{5}{9} \div \frac{7}{12} \square 2\frac{1}{3}$

b $\frac{2}{9} \div 1\frac{5}{6} \square \frac{5}{33}$

c $5\frac{1}{4} \div 1\frac{3}{8} \square 4$

d $7\frac{3}{16} \div 1\frac{3}{4} \square 4\frac{1}{14}$

DF **7** Write the answers to these in order of size. Start with the lowest number.

| $5\frac{1}{3} \div 1\frac{5}{6}$ | $4\frac{2}{5} \div 1\frac{1}{10}$ | $7\frac{7}{8} \div 2\frac{3}{4}$ | $10\frac{5}{12} \div 3\frac{1}{6}$ |

DF **8** Complete this multiplication grid.

×	$1\frac{2}{5}$	**b**
$3\frac{3}{4}$	**a**	$2\frac{1}{4}$
c	**d**	$5\frac{2}{3}$

DF **9** Work out these.

a $2\frac{1}{3} \times 3\frac{3}{7} \div 2\frac{4}{9}$

b $5\frac{3}{4} \div 2\frac{5}{8} \times 3\frac{1}{2}$

c $8\frac{2}{5} \div 2\frac{7}{10} \div 1\frac{4}{9}$

PB
ES **10** The diagram shows a rectangular wall.

The area of the wall is $5\frac{5}{9}$ m².

The width of the wall is $1\frac{2}{3}$ m.

Work out the perimeter of the wall.

PB
ES
11 Oleg has two boxes of soap powder. The soap powder is the same type in each box. Oleg puts the soap powder from these boxes into bags. Each bag contains $\frac{2}{5}$ kg of soap powder when full. He fills as many bags as possible.

On Saturday, Oleg sells all the bags of soap powder at a market. He makes 75p profit on each bag of soap powder he sells. How much profit did Oleg make in total?

$4\frac{2}{3}$ kg $3\frac{3}{7}$ kg

PB
ES
12 Ravi is going to put some lawn feed on his lawn. The total area of Ravi's lawn is 125 m². A packet of lawn feed covers $4\frac{5}{7}$ m² of lawn.

Each packet of lawn feed costs £1.89. Ravi thinks he can cover his lawn with lawn feed for less than £50. Is Ravi right? Show how you get your answer.

Lawn

Lawn

Number Strand 5 Percentages
Unit 3 Converting fractions and decimals to and from percentages

PS — PRACTISING SKILLS   DF — DEVELOPING FLUENCY   PB — PROBLEM SOLVING   ES — EXAM-STYLE

PS **1** Write these decimals as percentages.

   a 0.75

   b 0.25

   c 0.4

   d 0.38

   e 0.98

   f 0.165

   g 0.592

   h 0.06

PS **2** Write these percentages as decimals.

   a 75%

   b 18%

   c 90%

   d 5%

   e 29.5%

   f 7.4%

   g 156%

   h 0.14%

PS **3** Write these percentages as fractions in their simplest form.

   a 17%

   b 31%

   c 70%

   d 25%

e 20%

f 65%

g 72%

h 17.5%

PS **4** Write each fraction as a percentage.

a $\dfrac{41}{100}$

b $\dfrac{3}{10}$

c $\dfrac{4}{5}$

d $\dfrac{9}{20}$

e $\dfrac{17}{25}$

f $\dfrac{5}{8}$

g $\dfrac{9}{24}$

h $\dfrac{10}{32}$

DF **5** Write down, with reasons, which of these statements are true and which are false.

a $\dfrac{2}{5}$ is greater than 35%.

b 28% is equal to 0.28.

c $\dfrac{7}{9}$ is less than 75%.

d 0.65 is equal to $\dfrac{13}{20}$.

e $\dfrac{14}{35}$ is greater than 40%.

f 60% is less than $\dfrac{35}{56}$.

DF **6** A bag contains 50 counters. 27 of the counters are blue the rest are red.

a What fraction of the counters are blue?

b What percentage of the counters are blue?

c What percentage of the counters are red?

DF **7** Sally and Giles each took a language test. Sally got 17 out of 20 in her Spanish test. Giles got 13 out of 15 in his French test.

Who got the higher percentage in their language test, Sally or Giles?

DF **8** A weather forecaster says: 'There is an 85% probability of rain tomorrow.'

a Write 85% as a decimal.

b Write 85% as a fraction in its simplest form.

DF **9** The area of shape A is 54 cm². The area of shape B is 85 cm².

a Work out the area of shape A as a percentage of the area of shape B.

b Work out the area of shape B as a percentage of the area of shape A.

Give your answers to two decimal places.

DF **10** Henry saves coins in a jar. The diagram shows information about the coins in the jar.

a How many coins are there in the jar?

b What fraction of the coins are 20p coins?

c What percentage of the coins are 10p coins?

d Henry thinks that 35% of the coins are 5p coins. Is he right? Explain your answer.

DF **11** Work out the missing entries in the table. ●○○

Fraction	Decimal	Percentage
$\frac{2}{3}$	$0.\dot{6}$	**a**
$\frac{4}{9}$	**b**	$44.\dot{4}\%$
c	$0.\dot{3}$	$33.\dot{3}\%$
$\frac{5}{11}$	$0.\dot{4}\dot{5}$	**d**
$\frac{7}{22}$	**e**	$31.8\dot{1}\%$

DF **12** Write $\frac{7}{20}$, 40%, 0.3 and $\frac{11}{25}$ in order of size. Start with the smallest.

PB **13** Akemi plays tennis. She can win, lose or draw the games she plays.

ES Last year Akemi won 68% and lost $\frac{2}{7}$ of the games she played.

What percentage of the games did she draw? Give your answer correct to 2 decimal places.

PB **14** Which is greater $\frac{1}{3}$ or 30%? Give a reason for your answer. ●○○

ES

PB **15** Babs grows pink tulips, red tulips and white tulips. She says: '25% ●○○

ES of my tulips are pink, $\frac{9}{20}$ of my tulips are red and 0.35 of my tulips are white.'

Babs cannot be correct. Explain why.

Number Strand 5 Percentages Unit 4 Applying percentage increases and decreases to amounts

PS — PRACTISING SKILLS   DF — DEVELOPING FLUENCY   PB — PROBLEM SOLVING   ES — EXAM-STYLE

PS 1 Work out these.
- **a i** 1% of £250
  - **ii** 12% of £250
  - **iii** Decrease £250 by 12%.
- **b i** 1% of £21.50
  - **ii** 18% of £21.50
  - **iii** Decrease £21.50 by 18%.

PS 2 Work out these.
- **a** Decrease 350 g by 17%.
- **b** Increase 326 m by 21%.
- **c** Decrease £24.50 by 6%.
- **d** Increase 560 l by 12.5%.
- **e** Decrease 125 cm by 7.5%.
- **f** Increase $1250 by 3.5%.

PS 3 Kim buys a power drill for £68.50 plus VAT at 20%.
How much does she pay?

PS 4 Jose buys a plate for £24. He sells it the next day for a profit of 45%.
How much does Jose sell the plate for?

DF 5 Complete these. Which symbol, <, > or = goes in each box?
- **a** £350 increased by 10% ☐ £430 decreased by 10%
- **b** $49.50 decreased by 15% ☐ $52.40 decreased by 20%
- **c** €128 increased by 29% ☐ €132 increased by 26%
- **d** ₳1250 decreased by 15.8% ☐ ₳1100 increased by 7.5%

DF **6** Ravi travels to work by train. On Monday it took him 1 hour 40 minutes to travel to work. On Tuesday it took him 15% less time to travel to work.

How long did it take Ravi to travel to work on Tuesday?

DF **7** Yasmin has a meal at a restaurant. Here is her bill.

```
         Alf's Chip Shop
Fish and chips        £9.85
Tea                   £1.35
Subtotal a
15% service charge b
Total to pay c
```

Work out the missing entries in the bill.

PB
ES **8** The table gives information about the population of Riverton in 2005 and in 2015.

Marco says: 'The population of Riverton has increased by 10% from 2005 to 2015.' Is he right? Explain your answer.

Year	2005	2015
Population	15310	16678

PB
ES **9** Fiona works in a warehouse. For the first 20 hours she works in a week she is paid at an hourly rate of £7.80. For each additional hour she works her hourly rate is increased by 35%. Last week Fiona worked 28 hours.

Work out her pay.

PB
ES **10** Karl measures the lifetimes of two batteries, battery A and battery B. The lifetime of battery A was 36 hours. The lifetime of battery B was 48 hours. The manufacturer of the batteries claims that battery B lasts at least 30% longer than battery A.

Is the manufacturer correct? Explain your answer.

DF
ES **11** Chelsea invests £4800 at 2.4% per annum simple interest. Work out the total value of the investment after 3 years.

PB
ES **12** In the triangle ABC, angle CAB = 40° and angle ABC is 65% larger than angle CAB.

Work out angle BCA.

PB **13** The diagram shows two circles, circle P and circle Q. The area of circle P is 50 cm². The area of circle Q is 27.5% larger than the area of circle P.

Work out the radius of circle Q. Give your answer correct to 2 decimal places.

P
50 cm²

Q

Number Strand 5 Percentages
Unit 5 Finding the percentage change from one amount to another

PS PRACTISING SKILLS   **DF** DEVELOPING FLUENCY   **PB** PROBLEM SOLVING   **ES** EXAM-STYLE

PS **1** Work out these.

    a Write £2.75 as a percentage of £20.

    b Write 49.5°C as a percentage of 112.5°C.

    c Write 720 mm as a percentage of 960 mm.

    d Write 15.6 *l* as a percentage of 32.5 *l*.

    e Write 45° as a percentage of 360°.

    f Write 49.5 s as a percentage of 120 s.

PS **2** Write the first number as a percentage of the second number. Give each answer correct to 1 decimal place.

    a 2, 7

    b 17, 35

    c 27, 95

    d 29, 316

    e 359, 511

    f 511, 359

    g 18, 10.6

    h 0.789, 1.249

DF **3** Guy bought a car for £2400. The next day he sold the car for £3200.

    a How much profit did he make?

    b What is his percentage profit?

DF **4** Liam weighed 85 kg at the beginning of his diet and 77 kg at the end of his diet.

   a How much weight did he lose?

   b What is the percentage loss in his weight? Give your answer correct to 1 decimal place.

DF **5** The height of a tree at the beginning of the year is 17.5 m. The height of the tree at the end of the year is 18.9 m.

   Work out the percentage increase in the height of the tree.

PB **6** The diagram shows information about the counters in a bag.

ES   **a** Work out the percentage of blue counters in the bag.

   The percentage of black counters in the bag is greater than the percentage of green counters in the bag.

   b How much greater?

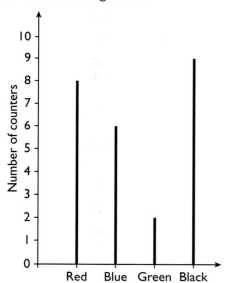

PB **7** A village collects £13 109 to build a new playground.

ES   The target is £20 000. The village magazine says: 'We've collected over 65% of our target, well done!'

   Is the village magazine right? Explain your answer.

PB
ES

8 The diagram gives information about the finances of a company.

   a What percentage of the company's finances is taxes?

The company director gets a bonus if the profit is 10% greater than the costs.

   b Does the company director get a bonus? Give a reason for your answer.

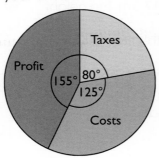

PB
ES

9 A box contains only arrow shapes and star shapes.

   a What percentage of the shapes are star shapes?

Ben is going to add some more arrow shapes to the box. He wants the percentage of arrow shapes in the box to equal 70%.

   b How many more arrow shapes does he need to add to the box?

PB
ES

10 The diagram shows the distances, in km, between some towns.

Laura is going to drive from Templeton to Tollercombe. The north route takes her through Whitchurch and Green Hill. The south route takes her through Thursk.

Work out the percentage increase in the length of her drive if she takes the north route rather than the south route. Give your answer correct to 1 decimal place.

Number Strand 6 Ratio and proportion Unit 2 Sharing in a given ratio

PS PRACTISING SKILLS   **DF** DEVELOPING FLUENCY   **PB** PROBLEM SOLVING   **ES** EXAM-STYLE

PS **1** Work these out.

   a Share 72 in the ratio 1:5.

   b Share 48 in the ratio 1:3.

   c Share 81 in the ratio 2:1.

   d Share 200 in the ratio 4:1.

PS **2** Work these out.

   a Share 60 in the ratio 2:3.

   b Share 91 in the ratio 3:4.

   c Share 105 in the ratio 5:2.

   d Share 250 in the ratio 7:3

PS **3** Work these out.

   a Share 54 in the ratio 1:3:2.

   b Share 90 in the ratio 5:2:3.

   c Share 117 in the ratio 2:3:4.

   d Share 425 in the ratio 1:1:3.

DF **4** Orange drink is made from orange concentrate and water in the ratio 1:14. Shelly makes some orange drink. She uses 25 ml of orange concentrate.

How much water does she need?

DF **5** A box of chocolates contains milk chocolates and plain chocolates in the ratio 3:4.

What fraction of the box of chocolates are

   a milk chocolates

   b plain chocolates?

DF **6** Haan and Ben win first prize in a tennis doubles competition. The first prize is £600. They share the prize in the ratio 7:5.

    a How much does Haan get?

    Haan now shares his part of the prize with Tania in the ratio 2:3

    b How much does Tania get?

DF **7** Emma and Joe share the cost of a meal in the ratio 2:5. The cost of the meal is £66.50. Joe pays more than Emma.

    How much more?

DF **8** A bag contains 20p coins and 50p coins in the ratio 7:5. There are a total of 180 coins in the bag.

    Work out the total amount of money in the bag.

DF **9** The area of pentagon A and the area of pentagon B are in the ratio 5:9. The area of pentagon A is 105 cm².

    Work out the area of pentagon B.

A
105 cm²

B

PB **10** A box contains red, blue and green counters in the ratio 2:4:3.

ES   **a** What fraction of the counters are blue?

    b What fraction of the counters are not red?

    There are 27 green counters in the bag.

    c Work out the total number of counters in the bag.

PB **11** Viki buys wooden chairs and plastic chairs in the ratio 3:7. The cost of each wooden chair is £31.60. The cost of each plastic chair is £15.80. The total cost of the wooden chairs is £284.40.

ES   How much does Viki pay in total for the plastic chairs?

PB **12** The angles in a triangle are in the ratio 2:3:7.

ES   Show that the triangle is not a right-angled triangle.

PB **13** A box contains only blue pens and black pens in the ratio 5:4. Olivia takes 8 blue pens from the box. The number of blue pens in the box is now equal to the number of black pens in the box.

    Work out the total number of pens in the box.

PB **14** The length and the width of a rectangle are in the ratio 5:3. The perimeter of the rectangle is 120 cm.

    Work out the area of the rectangle.

Number Strand 6 Ratio and proportion Unit 3 Working with proportional quantities

PS PRACTISING SKILLS   **DF** DEVELOPING FLUENCY   **PB** PROBLEM SOLVING   **ES** EXAM-STYLE

PS **1** Seven batteries cost a total of £8.75.

    a How much does 1 battery cost?

    b How much do 5 batteries cost?

PS **2** Twelve stamps cost a total of £6.96.

    a How much does 1 stamp cost?

    b How much do 17 stamps cost?

PS **3** Eight calculators cost a total of £46.80.

    a How much do 5 calculators cost?

    b How much do 13 calculators cost?

PS **4** There are a total of 252 matches in 7 identical boxes of matches. How many matches are there in

    a 5 boxes of matches

    b 11 boxes of matches?

PS **5** There are 180 packets of crisps in 5 boxes. How many packets of crisps are there in

    a 3 boxes

    b 8 boxes?

DF **6** Here is a recipe to make 12 almond shortbread biscuits. Grandma is going to use this recipe to make 21 biscuits. How much does she need of each ingredient?

Almond shortbread biscuits	
(makes 12 biscuits)	
5oz butter	8oz flour
1oz ground almonds	3oz caster sugar

DF **7** The label on a 0.75 *l* bottle of Fruit Squash says it makes 60 drinks.
What should the label on a 1.75 *l* bottle of Fruit Squash say about
the number of drinks it makes?

DF **8** Boxes of paperclips come in two sizes and prices.

    a For the small box of paperclips, work out the cost of 1 paperclip.

    b Which box is the better value for money? Explain your answer.

Small box

50 paperclips
£1.40

Large box

225 paperclips
£6.75

DF **9** For each of these, find the better value for money.
Explain your answers.

    a 5 rulers for £8 *or* 7 rulers for £10.50

    b 15 protractors for £10.20 *or* 12 protractors for £8.40

    c 13 compasses for £51 *or* 17 compasses for £66

DF **10** A spring stretches 6.3 cm when a force of 28 newtons (28 N) is applied to it.

    a How much will the spring stretch when a force of 15 N is
applied to it?

    The spring stretches 2.7 cm when a force *F* N is applied to it.

    b Work out the value of *F*.

PB **11** The table gives information about Mani's pay for last week.

ES This week Mani worked 30 hours at a standard rate and 10 hours
at a bonus rate.

How much more did he earn this week compared with last week?

	Number of hours worked	Total
Standard rate	35	£273.70
Bonus rate	5	£60.80
		£334.50

PB **ES** **12** Aabish is going to make some concrete. She has 100 kg of cement, 180 kg of sharp sand, 400 kg of aggregate and an unlimited supply of water.

Work out the greatest amount of concrete Aabish can make.

Materials for concrete	
(makes 0.125 m³)	
Cement	40 kg
Sharp sand	75 kg
Aggregate	150 kg
Water	22 *l*

PB **ES** **13** A parcel contains 12 large pies and 5 small pies. The total weight of the 12 large pies is 14.88 kg. The total weight of the 5 small pies is 4.25 kg.

John makes a different parcel. The parcel contains 8 large pies and 7 small pies.

a Work out the total weight of John's pies.

Jenny also makes a parcel. The parcel contains 7 large pies and some small pies. The total weight of all the pies in her parcel is 11.23 kg.

b Work out the number of small pies in Jenny's parcel.

PB **ES** **14** Baked beans come in three sizes of can. The table gives information about these cans.

Which size of can is the better value for money? Explain your answer.

Size of can	Weight of baked beans (grams)	Cost (p)
Small	180	28
Medium	415	64
Large	840	130

PB **15** The height of the Statue of Liberty is 305 feet. The height of St. Paul's Cathedral is 111 metres. (10 feet is approximately 3 metres)

Which is taller, the Statue of Liberty or St. Paul's Cathedral?

Algebra Strand 1 Starting Algebra Unit 4 Working with formulae

PS — PRACTISING SKILLS   DF — DEVELOPING FLUENCY   PB — PROBLEM SOLVING   ES — EXAM-STYLE

PS 1 Copy and complete the table for this number machine.

	Input	Output
a	20	
b		12
c	2	
d		−7
e	n	
f		p

PS 2 Copy and complete the table for this number machine.

	Input	Output
a	3	
b		56
c	0.5	
d		17
e	m	
f		q

DF **3** Angus thinks of a number. He multiplies the number by 5.
He then adds 3.

    a Work out the result if the number Angus thought of was

      i 2

      ii 10

      iii n.

    b Work out the number Angus thought of when the result was

      i 38

      ii 3

      iii p.

DF
PB
ES
4 £1 = €1.40 and £1 = \$1.60 are the exchange rates for the euro and the US dollar to pounds.

    a Change

      i £50 to euros

      ii \$50 to pounds

      iii €50 to US dollars.

    b A pair of sunglasses in Dublin cost €24.50. The same pair of sunglasses in Florida cost \$30. Work out the difference in the cost of these sunglasses.

DF **5** Here is a rule to change a quantity in litres into a quantity in pints.

> Multiply the number of litres by 1.75 to get the number of pints.

    a Change 40 litres to pints.

    b Change 1050 gallons to litres. 1 gallon = 8 pints.

DF
PB
ES
6 $A = \dfrac{bh}{2}$ is the formula to find the area of a triangle, where the base is b and the perpendicular height is h.

    a **i** Find A when $b = 5$ and $h = 7$.

      ii Find b when $A = 54$ and $h = 9$.

    b The area of a square is the same as the area of a triangle of base 25 and height 8. What is the length of each side of the square?

PB **7** Pamela hires a car. The cost £C, for the hire of a car for n days, in two different
ES garages, is shown in the boxes below.

Bill's Autos
$C = 11n + 60$

Carmart
$C = 20n$

a If Pamela hires a car for 8 days, show that Bill's Autos is the
cheaper of the two garages.

b For how many days would Pamela have to hire the car for
Carmart to be the cheaper garage?

DF **8** $P = 1.5x + 2y$ is a formula to work out the total cost £P of x cups
ES of tea and y cups of coffee.

a Work out the cost of 3 cups of tea and 5 cups of coffee.

b Peter buys 6 cups of tea and some cups of coffee. Work out
the number of cups of coffee if the total cost is £15.

PB **9** Here is a formula to change degrees centigrade, C, to
ES degrees Fahrenheit, F.

$$F = \frac{9C}{5} + 32$$

a On the 1st August, the temperature in New York was 79 °F.
On the 1st August, the temperature in Barcelona was 25 °C.
In which city was the temperature the greater?

b Show that –20 °C is a higher temperature than –5 °F.

c Work out the difference between 30 °C and 100 °F.

Algebra Strand 1 Starting Algebra Unit 5 Setting up and solving simple equations

PS — PRACTISING SKILLS   DF — DEVELOPING FLUENCY   PB — PROBLEM SOLVING   ES — EXAM-STYLE

PS **1** Solve the equations.

    a $a + 11 = 18$

    b $b - 3 = 9$

    c $5c = 65$

    d $7 = \dfrac{d}{4}$

PS **2** Solve the equations.

    a $3x - 2 = 13$

    b $5 - 4y = 17$

    c $2z + 15 = 7z + 9$

DF **3** Which of these equations does not have a solution $x = 3$?

    a $x + 5 = 8$

    b $7 - 2x = 1$

    c $\dfrac{10x}{6} = 5$

    d $1 - x = 4$

    e $2x - 5 = x - 2$

DF **ES** **4** Jen is x years old. Mary is twice as old as Jen. Rafa is 5 years older than Jen. The sum of their ages is 69 years.
How old will Rafa be in 10 years time?

PB **ES** **5** The lengths of the sides of a rectangle are given by $x + 1$, $3x - 2$, $9 - x$ and $x + 6$.
Work out the perimeter of the rectangle.

PB **ES** **6** Geoff pays £7.20 for 3 pies and 2 portions of chips.
Mel pays £4.50 for 5 portions of chips.
Sally buys 2 pies. How much does Sally pay?

PB **ES** **7** ABC is an isosceles triangle. Show that the greatest value for the perimeter of the triangle is 32.5.

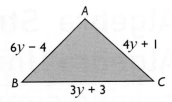

PB **ES** **8** Work out the size of the largest angle.

PB **ES** **9** Tom, Lucy and Sadiq share the driving on a journey of 145 miles. Tom drives x miles. Lucy drives three times as far as Tom. Sadiq drives 40 miles more than Lucy.

How many miles do they each drive?

PB **10** Ceri thinks of a number. She multiplies her number by 2 and then **ES** adds 3. Simon thinks of a number. He multiplies his number by 3 and then subtracts 2. Ceri and Simon both think of the same number.

What is the number they both thought of?

Algebra Strand 1 Starting Algebra Unit 6 Using brackets

PS — **PRACTISING SKILLS**   **DF** — **DEVELOPING FLUENCY**   **PB** — **PROBLEM SOLVING**   **ES** — **EXAM-STYLE**

PS **1** **a** Expand

    i $4(3m + 5)$

    ii $7(h - 3k)$.

   b Factorise

    i $12x - 8y$

    ii $6z + 6$.

PS **ES** **2** Orange juice costs £x per glass. Cola costs £y per glass. Ham sandwiches cost £a each. Cheese sandwiches cost £b each. Salad sandwiches cost £c each.

   a Sally, James and Hannah each have an orange juice and a cheese sandwich. Brian and Gary each have a cola and a salad sandwich. Write down an algebraic expression for the total cost.

   b Three different people each choose a drink and a sandwich. The total cost is $3y + 2a + c$. Write down what each had.

DF **ES** **3** Write down an expression for

   a the perimeter of this rectangle

   b the area of this rectangle.

Give your answers in their simplest form.

PS **4** **a** Expand

    i $3(b - 1) + 2(3 - b)$

    ii $5(a + 2) - 3(1 - a)$

   b Factorise

    i $6p^2 - 10p$

    ii $3c^2d + 9cd^2$.

DF
ES
5 Ella and Liam expand $2x(3x - 4)$.
This is what Ella wrote: $2x(3x - 4) = 6x^2 - 4$.
This is what Liam wrote: $2x(3x - 4) = 6x - 8x = -2x$.

  a Explain the mistake that each of Ella and Liam made.

  b Expand $2x(3x - 4)$.

PB
ES
6 CA, AB and BD are three sides of a quadrilateral
of side $(x + 2)$ cm. The fourth side, X, is twice as
long as the other three.
Show that the perimeter of the quadrilateral ABCD
can be written $5x + 10$.

PB
ES
7 Colin is n years old. Della is 4 years older than Colin. Ezra is twice
as old as Della.
Show that the sum of their ages is divisible by 4.

PB
ES
8 The cost of hiring a car is £C per day for the first 4 days.
The cost is £$(C - 5)$ per day for all additional days. Steve hires
a car for 10 days.

  a Write down an expression, in terms of C, for the total amount
Steve has to pay. Give your answer in its simplest form.

Anne pays £$4(3C - 10)$ for the hire of a car.

  b How many days did Anne hire a car for?

PB
ES
9 The diagram shows a path around three
sides of a lawn in a garden. The width of the
path is x metres. The garden is in the shape of
a rectangle of dimensions 20 m by 12 m.

Find, in terms of x, the perimeter of the lawn.
Give your answer in its simplest form.

PB
ES
10 Leanne thinks of a whole number. She adds 4 to her number and
then multiplies the result by 5. Isaac thinks of a whole number.
He subtracts 3 from his number and then multiplies the result by 8.
Show that Leanne and Isaac could not possibly have thought of
the same number.

Algebra Strand 2 Sequences
Unit 3 Linear sequences

PS — PRACTISING SKILLS   DF — DEVELOPING FLUENCY   PB — PROBLEM SOLVING   ES — EXAM-STYLE

DF ES 1 Here are the first four terms of a sequence.

2   7   12   17

Here are the first four terms of another sequence.

4   7   10   13

The number 7 is in both sequences.

a Find the next two numbers that are in both sequences.

John says the number 202 is in both sequences.

b Is John right?

DF ES 2 Here are Pattern number 3 and Pattern number 4 of a sequence of patterns.

Pattern number 3   Pattern number 4

a Draw Pattern number 1 and Pattern number 2.

b Find the missing numbers in the table for this sequence of patterns.

Pattern number	1	2	3	4	5	10
Number of dots			8	11		

3 Here are the 2nd, 4th and 5th terms of a sequence.

___   15   ___   27   33

DF **a** Write down the 1st and 3rd terms of this sequence.

ES **b** Work out the product of the 6th and 7th terms of this sequence.

Ruth says that all the terms in this sequence are odd numbers.

PB **c** Show that Ruth is right.

PB **ES** **4** The anchor on a boat is lowered 3 metres with each turn of a handle. The anchor is already 5 metres below the surface of the sea.

   a How many metres below the surface of the sea will the anchor be after n turns of the handle?

The anchor hits the bottom of the sea after 64 turns of the handle.

   b How deep is the sea?

DF **ES** **5** Find the missing numbers in the table for this pattern of stars made with matchsticks.

Number of stars	1	2	3	4	8	20	n
Number of matches	10	19	28				

PB **ES** **6** A machine makes parts for a mobile phone. The list shows the number of parts that are made at 1 p.m. and at every 5 minutes after 1 p.m.

   240   265   290   315   340

How many parts will be made at 2.30 p.m?

7 Here are the first four terms of a sequence.

   150   138   126   114

PS   **a** Write down the next two terms in this sequence.

PB   **b** In what position is the first negative number in this sequence?

ES   **c** Show that the nth term of this sequence can be written in the form $6(a + bn)$.

PB **ES** **8** Here are the first five terms of a sequence.

   3   7   11   15   19

   a **i** Write down the next two terms in this sequence.

      ii Explain how you got your answer to part **i**.

   b Find the 15th term of this sequence.

   c Write down, in terms of n, the nth term of this sequence.

PB **ES** **9** The nth term of sequence A is $2n + 1$. The nth term of sequence B is $4n - 3$.

   a How many of the first 10 numbers in sequence A are prime numbers?

   b Show that the sum of all corresponding numbers in each sequence is always an even number.

Algebra Strand 2 Sequences
Unit 4 Special sequences

DF **1** Here are the first eight terms of a sequence.

0   2   2   4   6   10   16   26

a Describe the rule for working out the terms in this sequence.

b Johan says: 'All the terms in this sequence must be even numbers.' Explain why Johan is right.

c What is special about these numbers?

PS
ES **2** Here are the first three patterns in a sequence of patterns.

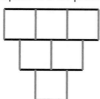

a Write down the first 5 terms in the sequence formed by the vertical lines.

b Show that the nth term of this sequence can be written as $\dfrac{n(n+3)}{2}$.

PS
ES **3** The thickness of a piece of paper is 0.04 mm. Megan cuts the piece of paper in half. She places the pieces in a pile. Megan then cuts each piece of paper in the pile in half. She then places all the pieces in a pile. Megan continues to do this.

a Work out the height of the pile after Megan has done this 5 times.

b **i** Work out the height of the pile after Megan has done this 20 times.

   ii Explain why your answer to part **i** does not make sense.

4 Here is a sequence made from equilateral triangles.

    Pattern 1 is a 1 × 1 × 1 equilateral triangle

    Pattern 2 is a 2 × 2 × 2 equilateral triangle

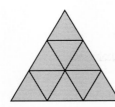   Pattern 3 is a 3 × 3 × 3 equilateral triangle

a Draw Pattern 4 and describe this equilateral triangle.
b i Write down the sequence of grey triangles.
 ii Describe this sequence.
c i How many triangles are in Pattern 4?
 ii Write down an expression, in terms of n, for the number of grey triangles in Pattern n.

PB
ES **5** Here is a sequence of patterns made with dots and straight lines.

Pattern 1   Pattern 2   Pattern 3

a Find the missing numbers in the table.

Pattern number	1	2	3	4	10
Number of dots	4	9			
Number of lines	5	15			
Number of triangles	2	6			

b Write down, in terms of n, the nth term for the sequence of dots.
c i Show that the nth term for the sequence of triangles is $n^2 + n$.
 ii Use $n^2 + n$ to help you write, in terms of n, the nth term for the sequence of lines.

PB **ES** **6** Here are the first three terms of a sequence.

1   3   7

Alan says the next term in this sequence is 13. Becky says the next term in this sequence is 15.

a Explain how **both** Alan and Becky could be right.

b **i** Write down the 5th term of Alan's sequence.

ii Write down the 5th term of Becky's sequence.

PB **ES** **7** Here are the first four terms of a sequence.

16   8   4   2

a Write down the next three terms of this sequence.

b Which of the following expressions is the nth term of this sequence?

$$\frac{32}{2^{n+1}} \qquad \frac{n}{2} \qquad 2n \qquad \frac{32}{2^{n-1}} \qquad \frac{32}{2^n}$$

PB **ES** **8** P_n is the perimeter of an equilateral triangle. The next equilateral triangle is formed by joining the midpoints of the triangle. This is shown in the diagram.

$P_1 = 3s$

Write down P_2, P_3, P_4 and P_5 in terms of s.

Algebra Strand 3 Functions and graphs Unit 1 Real-life graphs

PS - PRACTISING SKILLS   DF - DEVELOPING FLUENCY   PB - PROBLEM SOLVING   ES - EXAM-STYLE

PS
ES

1 Electra is collecting information about the price of one litre of petrol in a 6-month period. Draw a line graph to show this information.

Month	Jan	Feb	Mar	Apr	May	Jun
Price in pence	112	115	117	115	116	118

PS
ES

2 You can use this graph to change between pounds and kilograms.

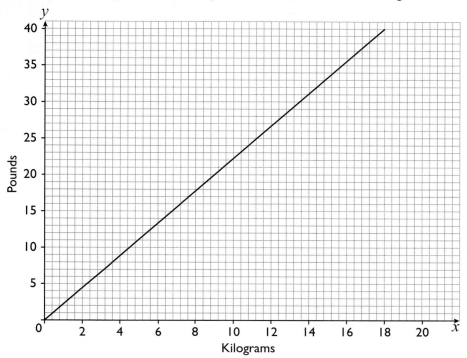

a Change 15 pounds to kilograms.

b Change 10 kilograms to pounds.

> 1 stone = 14 pounds

PB

c James weighs 12 stone 12 pounds. Iram weighs 80 kilograms.
Who is the heavier, James or Iram?

DF **3** David recorded the temperature at midday each day for a week. The diagram
shows some information about his results.

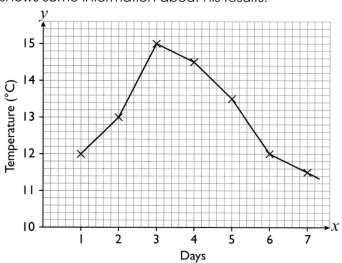

61

a Write down the range of the midday temperatures for this week.

b Between which two days was the change in temperature the greatest?

c Work out the average temperature for this week.

PB **4** Katie travelled 20 km from
ES home to a furniture shop.
She then spent some time
in the shop before
returning home. This travel
graph shows part of her
journey.

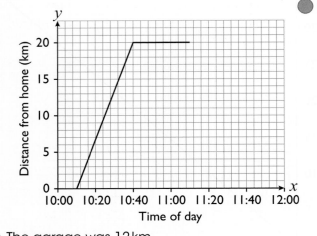

a Write down Katie's
distance from the
furniture shop at 10:20.

Katie left the shop at
11:10 to return home.
On the way, at 11:30,
she stopped for
10 minutes at a garage. The garage was 12 km
from her home. Katie arrived home at 12:00.

b **i** Work out Katie's average speed from the garage to her home.

ii At which part of the whole journey did Katie travel the quickest?

PB **5** This graph can be used to change between pounds (£)
ES and US dollars ($).

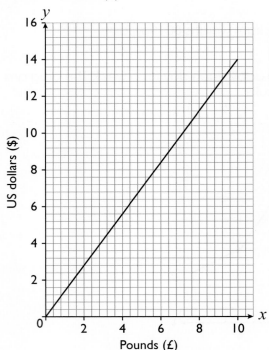

a Use the graph to change £5 to US dollars.

A laptop in the UK costs £460. The same model in the US costs $720.

b Where is the laptop the cheapest?

PB
ES
6 This conversion graph can be used to change between litres and gallons. There are 8 pints in 1 gallon.

A dairy farm produces 720 pints of milk each day. The farmer sells the milk for 32p per litre.

How much money does the farmer sell his milk for each week?

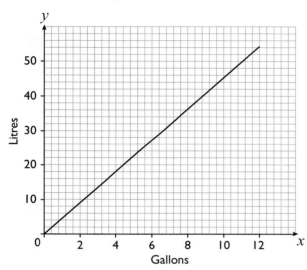

DF
ES
7 Rosa travelled from her home to her friend's house 40 km away. She stayed for some time at her friend's house before returning home. Rosa left home at 10:10. She travelled at an average speed of 80 km/h. She stayed at her friend's house for half an hour. Rosa arrived home at 11:40.

Draw a travel graph to show Rosa's journey.

PB
8 Describe a situation that could be represented by this speed/time graph.

Algebra Strand 3 Functions and graphs Unit 2 Plotting graphs of linear functions

PS — PRACTISING SKILLS   DF — DEVELOPING FLUENCY   PB — PROBLEM SOLVING   ES — EXAM-STYLE

DF **1** Milk is sold at 90p per litre.

   a Work out the missing values in this table.

Number of litres	1	2	5	10	20	50	100
Cost in £	0.90			9			90

   b Draw a graph to show this information about the cost of milk.

   c Find the cost of 30 litres of milk.

   d How many litres of milk can be bought for £20?

DF
ES **2** Lisa's company pays her travel expenses for each mile she travels.

   a Work out the missing values in this table.

Miles travelled	5	10	15	20	25	30	35	40
Expenses in £	4	8		16			28	

   b Draw a graph to show this information.

   c Lisa travels 28 miles. Work out how much her company pays her.

   d Lisa's company paid her £60 in travel expenses. How many miles did Lisa travel?

PB
ES **3** This is a table of values for $y = \frac{1}{2}x + 5$.

x	−2	−1	0	1	2	3	4
y		4.5	5				7

   a Complete the table of values.

   b Using 2 mm graph paper, draw the graph of $y = \frac{1}{2}x + 5$.

     Use values of x-axis −2 to 4, and values of y-axis −1 to 8.

PB **4** This rule can be used to work out the time, in seconds, it takes
ES to download music tracks.

> Time = 25 × number of music tracks + 10

a Work out the missing information in this table of values.

Number of tracks	2	4	6		10	12
Time in seconds	60			210		

b Draw a graph to show the time it takes to download music tracks.

c How many tracks can be downloaded in 10 minutes?

PB **5** Vijay lives 3 kilometres from his school. The travel graph shows
ES Vijay's journey to school one day.

a Describe the three stages in Vijay's journey to school.

On another day, Vijay left home at 08:15. At 08:32 he stopped at
a shop to buy a drink. The shop is 1.4 km from school.
At 08:38 he left the shop and carried on walking to school.
He arrived at school at 08:45.

b Draw a travel graph to show this journey.

PB **6** This is a table of values for $y = 3x + 4$.
ES

x	−2	−1	0	1	2	3
y		1				13

a Work out the missing values for this table.

b Use your table to draw the graph of $y = 3x + 4$ from $x = -2$ to $x = 3$.

c Find the value of x when $y = 8$.

PB
ES
7 Peter goes on holiday to Prague. The currency in Prague is the Czech Crown (czk). The exchange rate is £1 = 30czk.

    a Draw a graph that could be used to convert between £ (pounds) and czk (Czech Crown).

Peter bought a suitcase in Prague. He paid 750czk for the suitcase. In London the same model of suitcase costs £34.

    b How much money did Peter save by buying the suitcase in Prague?

PB
ES
8 Here is a rule to work out the cost, in pounds, of printing invitations at Printshop.

> Cost (£C) = number of invitations (n) × 1.25 + 4

    a Write down a formula for C in terms of n.

    b Draw a graph of C against n.

At Print-4-U, the cost is £20 for printing 12 of each invitation. Martin wants 24 invitations printed.

    c Which shop should Martin buy his invitations from?

PB
ES
9 Pat delivers parcels. The table shows the cost of delivering parcels for different journeys.

Distance in miles	10	20	30	40	50
Cost in £	20	30	40	50	60

    a Draw a graph to show this information.

For each parcel Pat delivers there is a fixed charge plus a charge for each mile.

    b Use your graph to work out the fixed charge and the charge for each mile.

Vanessa also delivers parcels. For each parcel Vanessa delivers it costs £1.50 for each mile. There is no fixed charge.

    c Compare the cost of having a parcel delivered by Pat with the cost of having a parcel delivered by Vanessa.

DF
ES
10 Draw the graph of $y = 2x + 3$ for values of x from $x = -3$ to $x = 1$.

Algebra Strand 3 Functions and graphs Unit 3 The equation of a straight line

PS PRACTISING SKILLS   **DF** DEVELOPING FLUENCY   **PB** PROBLEM SOLVING   **ES** EXAM-STYLE

PS **1** Here are some lines drawn on a co-ordinate grid.

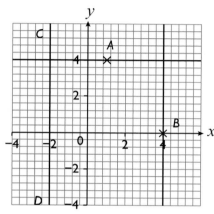

a Write down the equation of

   i the horizontal line passing through A

   ii the vertical line passing through B

   iii the line CD.

b Draw the lines with equation

   i $x = 2.5$

   ii $y = -3$.

PB
ES **2** Here are equations of two lines.

   $y = 1.5x - 4$ $3x - 2y = 4$

Brian says the two lines are parallel. Jane says the two lines have the same y-intercept.

a Who is right, Brian or Jane, or are they both right?

b Write down the gradient of $y = 1.5x - 4$.

PB **3** Here are some lines drawn on a co-ordinate grid.

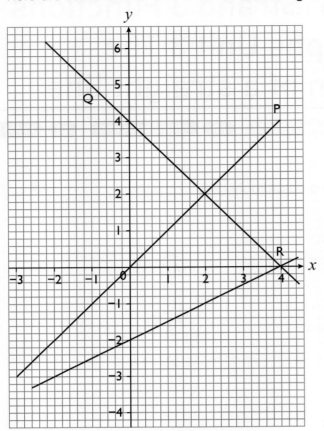

a Write down an equation for

i P

ii Q

iii R.

b On a copy of the grid, draw the lines with equations

i $y = 3x$

ii $x - y = 3$.

PB
ES
4 The diagram shows the line PQ. A line, L, is parallel to PQ and passes through the point (9, 0). Find an equation of the line L.

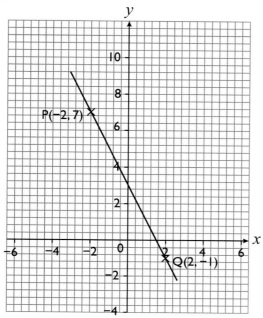

PB
ES
5 This graph shows the cost (£C) Parcelsend charge for sending parcels weighing w kg.

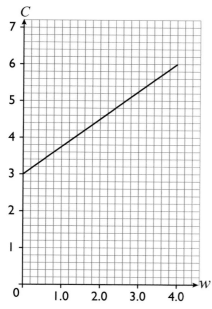

a Write down an equation of this line.

Send-by-Post use the equation $C = 2w$ to work out their charges for sending parcels. Lev wants to send a parcel of weight 2.5 kg.

b Which company should Lev use, Parcelsend or Send-by-Post?

PB **ES** **6** A is a point with co-ordinates (5, 3). B is a point with co-ordinates (3, –7). ●●○

   a Work out an equation of a straight line passing through A and B.
   Another straight line, L, has y intercept of 1. L is parallel to AB.

   b Find an equation of L.

DF **ES** **7** Here is a sketch of the graph of $2x + 3y = 6$. ●●○

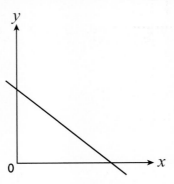

   a Write down the co-ordinates of the point where the line crosses the x-axis.

   b Find the gradient of the line.

   c Does this line pass through the point with co-ordinates (2, 0.5)?

PB **ES** **8** The line, M, passes through the point (–2, 5). It is parallel to the line with equation $x + y = 5$. ●●○

   a Find an equation of the line M.
   The line with equation $y = 2x$ intersects M at the point B.

   b Work out the co-ordinates of the point B.

   c Find the value of x when $y = 8$.

Algebra Strand 3 Functions and graphs Unit 4 Plotting quadratic and cubic graphs

PS — PRACTISING SKILLS   **DF** — DEVELOPING FLUENCY   **PB** — PROBLEM SOLVING   **ES** — EXAM-STYLE

PS **1 a** This is a table of values for $y = x^2 + 3x - 5$. Work out the missing values in the table.

x	–3	–2	–1	0	1	2	3	4
y	–5			–5		5		

b This is a table of values for $y = 1 + 2x - 3x^2$. Work out the missing values in the table.

x	–3	–2	–1	0	1	2	3	4
y		–15			0			–39

PS **2 a** This is a table of values for $y = x^3 - x + 4$. Work out the missing values in the table.

x	–3	–2	–1	0	1	2	3	4
y		–2		4	4			64

b This is a table of values for $y = 2x^3 - 6x^2 + 3x - 1$. Work out the missing values in the table.

x	–3	–2	–1	0	1	2	3	4
y			–12		–2		8	

DF **3** The diagram shows part of the graph of $y = 2x^2 - x - 6$.

a Write down the co-ordinates of the y-intercept.

b Write down the solutions of the equation $2x^2 - x - 6 = 0$.

c By considering the line $y = -3$, estimate the solutions of the equation $2x^2 - x - 3 = 0$.

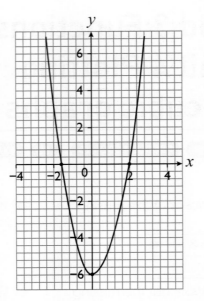

DF **4** The diagram shows part of the graph of $y = x^3 - 2x^2 - 3x$.

    a Write down the solutions of the equation $x^3 - 2x^2 - 3x = 0$.

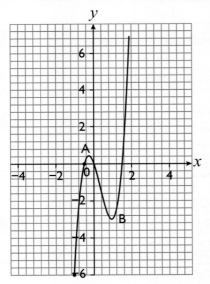

    b Estimate the co-ordinates of the points A and B.

    c Show that the equation $x^3 - 2x^2 - 3x = 4$ has just one solution.

DF ES 5 This is a table of values for $y = x^2 - 2x - 3$.

x	-3	-2	-1	0	1	2	3	4
y		5		-3				5

    a Work out the missing values in the table.

    b Draw a graph of $y = x^2 - 2x - 3$.

    c Use your graph to solve $x^2 - 2x - 3 = 0$.

    d Estimate solutions of the equation $x^2 - 2x - 5 = 0$.

DF ES 6 This is a table of values for $y = x^3 - 2x^2 - 5x + 6$.

x	-3	-2	-1	0	1	2	3	4
y				6			0	

    a Work out the missing values in the table.

    b Draw a graph of $y = x^3 - 2x^2 - 5x + 6$.

    c Use your graph to solve $x^3 - 2x^2 - 5x + 6 = 0$.

DF ES 7 a Draw a graph of $y = 3 + x - 4x^2$.

    b Use your graph to solve $3 + x - 4x^2 = 0$.

    c Estimate solutions of the equation $3 + x - 4x^2 = 0$.

DF ES 8 On the same axes, draw graphs of $y = x^3 - x$ and $y = x$.
The graphs cross at points A, B and C.

    a Write down the co-ordinates of points A, B and C.

    b The x-co-ordinates of A, B and C are the solutions of a cubic
equation. Write down this equation.

    c Write down the equation of a straight line you could draw
to solve $x^3 - 3x = 3$.

PB ES 9 A cricket ball is thrown vertically up from 2 metres above
the ground. Its path is modelled by the quadratic function
$h = 2 + 9t - 5t^2$ where h is the height of the ball and t the time.

    a Draw the graph of h against t for values of t from 0 to 2 at
intervals of 0.25.

    b Use your graph to find the greatest height the ball reaches
from the ground.

Geometry and Measures
Strand 1 Units and scales
Unit 8 Bearings

PS PRACTISING SKILLS   **DF** DEVELOPING FLUENCY   **PB** PROBLEM SOLVING   **ES** EXAM-STYLE

PS **1** Answer these.

    a Measure the bearing of Oxford from Bath.

    b Measure the bearing of Bath from Oxford.

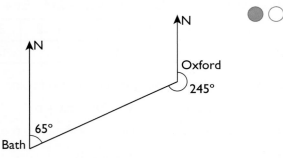

PS **2** **a** Write down the bearing of these compass directions.

      i West

      ii South-East.

    b Write down the compass points with these bearings.

      i 090°

      ii 225°.

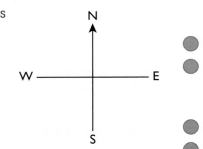

DF
ES **3** The diagram shows two coastguard stations, P and Q. The bearing of Q from P is 080°. There is a boat at point B. The bearing of B from P is 140°. The bearing of B from Q is 240°. Find the angle PBQ.

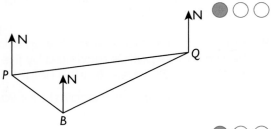

PB
ES **4** An aeroplane flew 60 km from A to B, then 80 km from B to C, and then back from C to A. The bearing of B from A is 120°. The bearing of C from B is 270°.

    a Using a scale of 1 cm to represent 10 km, draw an accurate diagram to show the aeroplane's journey.

    b **i** What bearing must the aeroplane travel on to get from C to A?

      ii What is the distance from C to A?

DF 5 Ipswich is on a bearing of 080° from Sudbury.

ES
    a What is the bearing of Sudbury from Ipswich?
Ipswich is also North-East of Colchester.

    b Find the bearing of Ipswich from Colchester.

    c Work out the back bearing of Colchester from Ipswich.

DF 6 The diagram shows a ship, S, and its position from two lighthouses, P and Q.
Find the bearing of

    a P from Q

    b S from P

    c Q from P

    d P from S.
Q is South-West of S.

    e Find the bearing of S from Q.

PB 7 Ben sails his boat from Cromer on a bearing of 060° for 6 km.
He then changed direction and sailed on a bearing of 150° for 8 km.

ES
    a Draw an accurate diagram to show Ben's boat trip. Use a scale of 1 cm to represent 1 km.

Ben then travels back to Cromer along a straight line.

    b What bearing does Ben travel on to get back to Cromer?

    c How far does he travel in total?

PB 8 Four buoys A, B, C and D are arranged so that

ES
        B is on a bearing of 60° from A
        C is on a bearing of 105° from A
        C is on a bearing of 150° from B
        A is on a bearing of 330° from D.
Explain why ABCD is a square.

PB 9 A plane is travelling due South at 200 miles an hour. At 10 a.m.

ES
the bearing of an island from the plane is 120°. At 10.30 a.m.
the bearing of the island from the plane is 060°. The plane will
not pass within 75 miles of the island. Explain why.

Geometry and Measures
Strand 1 Units and scales
Unit 9 Scale drawing

PS — **PRACTISING SKILLS**   **DF** — **DEVELOPING FLUENCY**   **PB** — **PROBLEM SOLVING**   **ES** — **EXAM-STYLE**

PS **ES** **1** A map has a scale of 1:25000. The distance between the church and the garage in a village is 2 cm on the map.

    a Work out the actual distance between the church and the garage.

    The actual distance between two petrol stations is 4 km.

    b How far apart are the petrol stations on the map?

DF **2** Rosie follows these instructions when she takes part in an orienteering competition.

       Start at the town clock and walk North for 200 metres.

       Walk East for 150 metres and then South for 100 metres.

    a Use a scale of 1 cm represents 20 m to draw a scale drawing of Rosie's walk.

    b How far is Rosie from her starting point?

DF **ES** **3** Judy wants to find the length of the sloping roof of the end of her shed. She cannot reach the top of the shed so draws a scale drawing of the end of the shed.

    Find the length of the slope.

DF **4** Here is an accurate plan of a garden drawn on a scale of 1 cm represents 4 m.

    Copy and complete the table to show the actual measurements of the garden.

Measurement	Drawing	Actual
Length of lawn		
Width of lawn		
Radius of pond		
Width of veg plot		
Length of patio		
Width of patio		

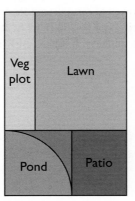

DF ES 5 Tyson wants to draw a scale drawing of the town gardens. ● ○ ○
He is going to use a sheet of paper that is 70 cm long by 44 cm wide.
The town gardens are rectangular in shape and have a length of
280 m and a width of 150 m.

Explain what scale Tyson should use to make his scale drawing
as large as possible.

PB ES 6 Here is a 3-D sketch of the extension Ellie wants to ● ○ ○
add to her house. The overall height of the
extension must be 4.3 m.

Using a scale drawing, find the height of
the wall.

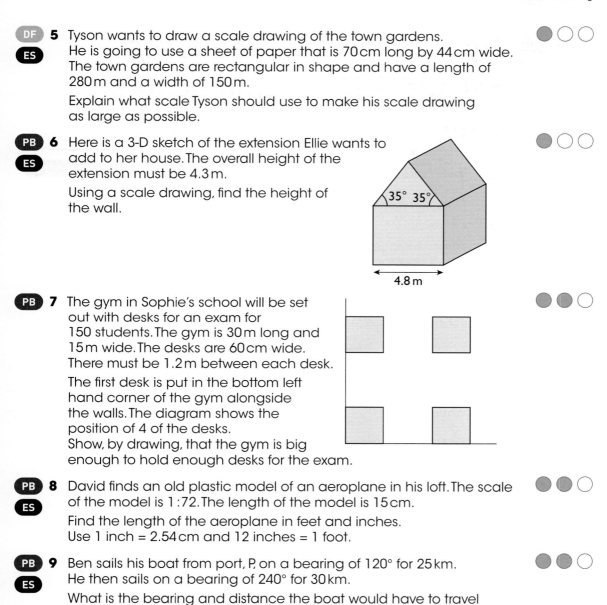

35° 35°

4.8 m

PB 7 The gym in Sophie's school will be set ● ● ○
out with desks for an exam for
150 students. The gym is 30 m long and
15 m wide. The desks are 60 cm wide.
There must be 1.2 m between each desk.

The first desk is put in the bottom left
hand corner of the gym alongside
the walls. The diagram shows the
position of 4 of the desks.
Show, by drawing, that the gym is big
enough to hold enough desks for the exam.

PB ES 8 David finds an old plastic model of an aeroplane in his loft. The scale ● ● ○
of the model is 1 : 72. The length of the model is 15 cm.

Find the length of the aeroplane in feet and inches.
Use 1 inch = 2.54 cm and 12 inches = 1 foot.

PB ES 9 Ben sails his boat from port, P, on a bearing of 120° for 25 km. ● ● ○
He then sails on a bearing of 240° for 30 km.

What is the bearing and distance the boat would have to travel
in order to get back to port P?

Geometry and Measures
Strand 1 Units and scales
Unit 10 Compound units

PS PRACTISING SKILLS   **DF** DEVELOPING FLUENCY   **PB** PROBLEM SOLVING   **ES** EXAM-STYLE

PS **1** Work these out.

    a Natalie drove at an average speed of 44 mph for two and a half hours. Work out how far she travelled.

    b Jason drove 330 km in 6 hours. Work out his average speed.

    c Bavna walked from her home to school at an average speed of 4.5 km/h. The school was 1.5 km from her home. Work out how long it took her.

PS **2** Mike ran 100 m in 9.8 seconds.

ES   **a** Work out his average speed in m/s.

    b Change your answer to km/h.

PS **3** Gareth's car uses 5 litres of petrol when it travels 30 miles.

ES   Susan's car uses 8 litres of petrol when it travels 50 miles.

   Whose car has the higher average rate of petrol consumption?

DF **4** Becca is going to grow a new lawn from seed. Her lawn is a

ES   rectangle 17 m long and 5 m wide. She buys a 2 kg box of grass seed which is enough to grow a 100 m² lawn.

   How many grams of grass seed will she have left?

DF **5** Toni's train leaves Bath railway station at 09:15. It arrives in London

ES   at 10:30. It travels 120 miles from Bath to London.

   Work out its average speed in mph.

DF **6** The speed of light is 186 000 miles per second. The Sun is 93 million

ES   miles from the Earth.

   Work out how long it takes a ray of light to travel from the Sun to the Earth. Give your answer in minutes and seconds.

PB **7** The speed limit on motorways in France is 130 km/h. The speed

ES   limit on motorways in the UK is 70 mph.

   Find the difference in the two speed limits. Use the fact that 5 miles = 8 km.

PB
ES
8 Sophie has a fish pond in the shape of a cuboid. She needs to empty the full pond to clean it out.

She puts all the fish into another pond and pumps the water out at a rate of 25 litres per minute. She starts pumping out the water at 10 a.m.
At what time will the pond be empty?
Use the fact that $1\,m^3 = 1000$ litres.

PB
ES
9 Mia is going to visit her mother who lives 230 miles away. She drives at an average speed of 60 mph for an hour and a half. She then stops for a 15 minute rest. She travels the remaining part of the journey at an average speed of 70 mph.

Work out Mia's overall average speed for the whole journey.

PB
10 Stuart uses this conversion graph to change between litres and gallons.

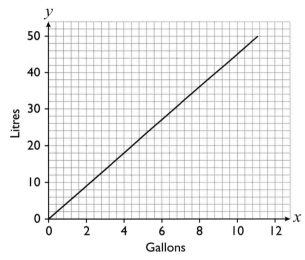

a i   Change 5 gallons to litres.
ii Change 45 litres to gallons.

Stuart uses on average 0.5 litres of heating oil per hour to run his heating system. The heating system works for 14.5 hours a day for 200 days of the year. Stuart has two empty tanks in which he stores the heating oil. Tank P holds 1000 litres of oil. Tank Q holds 300 gallons of oil.
Stuart buys enough heating oil to last a whole year. He completely fills Tank P and puts the rest of the oil into Tank Q.

b How many gallons does Stuart put into tank Q?

Stuart decides to completely fill up tank Q as he gets a special deal on heating oil. The extra oil costs 32p per litre.

c How much does it cost to completely fill Tank Q?

Geometry and Measures
Strand 2 Properties of shapes
Unit 6 Types of quadrilateral

PS — PRACTISING SKILLS   **DF** — DEVELOPING FLUENCY   **PB** — PROBLEM SOLVING   **ES** — EXAM-STYLE

PS **1** Name the quadrilaterals that have

    a two pairs of opposite sides equal and parallel

    b four equal sides

    c diagonals that cross at 90°.

PS **2** **a** Draw a trapezium that has one acute angle only.

    b Draw a kite that has one right angle only.

    c Draw an arrowhead that has one right angle only.

    d Explain why it is not possible to draw a trapezium with only one
right angle.

DF **3** Draw an xy co-ordinate grid with x- and y-axes from 0 to 8.

    a Plot the points P at (2, 8) and Q at (6, 5).

      i Draw a rectangle with PQ as a diagonal.

    b Plot the point, R, at (7, 1).

      i Find the co-ordinates of S to make PQRS a parallelogram.

DF **4** Draw an xy co-ordinate grid with x-and y-axes from –2 to 8.

    a Plot the points A at (7, 2) and C at (1, 6).

      i Draw a rhombus with AC as a diagonal.

    b Plot the point B at (5, 6).

      i Find the co-ordinates of a possible position of D to make
ABCD an isosceles trapezium.

DF **5** PQRS is a parallelogram.

    Find the missing angles P, Q and R of
the parallelogram. Explain your answer.

PB **ES** **6** ABCD is an isosceles trapezium. BEC is an isosceles triangle.

AD = BC = CE

Find the size of angle D. Give reasons for your answer.

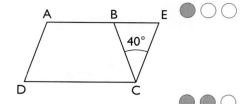

PB **ES** **7** EFGH is a rhombus. JHG is a straight line.

Explain why angle EGF is 64°.

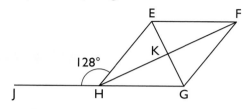

PB **ES** **8** ABCD is a rhombus.

P is the midpoint of AB.
Q is the midpoint of BC.
R is the midpoint of CD.
S is the midpoint of DA.
Explain why PQRS is a rectangle.

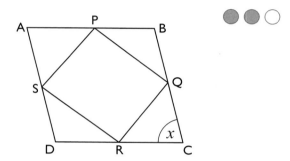

PB **ES** **9** PQST is a parallelogram. QRS is an isosceles triangle.

Work out the size of angle SQR. Give reasons for your answer.

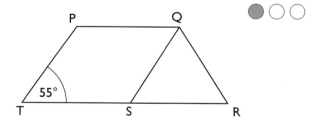

PB **ES** **10** ABCE is a parallelogram. ADE is a right-angled triangle.

Work out the size of angle EAD. Give reasons for your answer.

81

Geometry and Measures
Strand 2 Properties of shapes
Unit 7 Angles and parallel lines

PS – PRACTISING SKILLS   **DF** – DEVELOPING FLUENCY   **PB** – PROBLEM SOLVING   **ES** – EXAM-STYLE

PS **1** Write down the name of the marked angles.   ● ○ ○

a

b

c

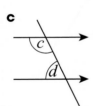

PS **2** Find the missing angles in these diagrams.   ● ○ ○
Give reasons for your answer.

a

b

PS **3** Find the missing angles in these diagrams.

a

b

PS **4** Explain fully why the two allied (co-interior) angles marked
on this diagram are supplementary.

DF **5** Here is a diagram of a gate.
Find the missing angles. Give reasons for your answer.

DF **6** PQRS is a rectangle. SRT is a straight line. PQTR is a parallelogram.
ES Find the value of angle RPS.

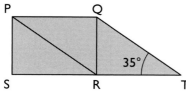

DF **7** ABDE is a parallelogram. BCD is an isosceles triangle.
ES Find the size of angle AED. Give reasons for your answer.

PB **ES** **8** The diagram is made up from a rectangle and a parallelogram.
Find the size of the angle marked a.

PB **ES** **9** EFG is an isosceles triangle. Explain why.

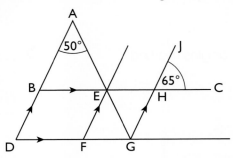

PB **ES** **10 a** Use this diagram to explain why the three angles of a triangle add up to 180°. You must give reasons with your explanation.

b Write down a fact in your explanation.

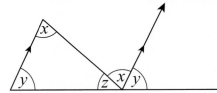

PB **ES** **11** Explain why AB and CD are parallel lines. Give reasons for each step of your explanation.

Geometry and Measures
Strand 2 Properties of shapes
Unit 8 Angles in a polygon

PS — PRACTISING SKILLS   DF — DEVELOPING FLUENCY   PB — PROBLEM SOLVING   ES — EXAM-STYLE

PS 1 Work out the size of the exterior angle and the interior angle of these regular shapes. ●○○

a

b

PS 2 Find the number of sides in a regular polygon that has an ●○○
   a exterior angle of 20°
   b interior angle of 108°.

DF **3** The interior angle of a regular polygon is 140°. Find the number of ●○○
ES sides in the polygon.

140°
140°

PB **4** Find the size of angle x. ●○○
ES

110°   30°

x

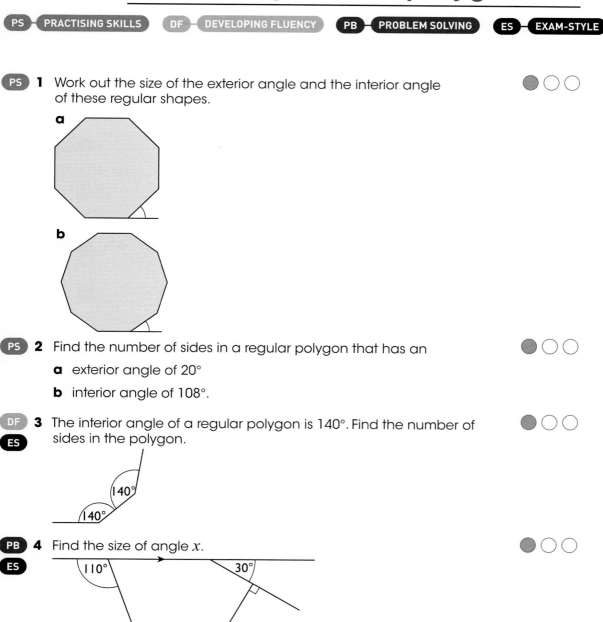

PB **ES** **5** The diagram shows a regular octagon and a regular hexagon.
Find the size of the angle marked m.

PB **ES** **6** Here is a regular dodecagon, centre O.
Explain why OPQ makes
an equilateral triangle.

PS **ES** **7** Here is a regular octagon. Two of its
diagonals are drawn on the
shape. Find the size of angle p.

DF **ES** **8** The sum of the interior angles of a polygon is 2340°. Work out the
number of sides in the polygon.

DF **ES** **9** Three regular polygons meet at a point.
One of the polygons has an interior
angle of 60°. Another polygon has an
interior angle of 144°.

Find the number of sides in each of
the three polygons.

PB **ES** **10** The diagram shows a regular heptagon
and a regular pentagon drawn on the same
base. Work out the size of the angle marked t.

PB **ES** **11** Explain, giving reasons, why it is possible to tile a floor using regular
dodecagons and equilateral triangles that have the same length side.
You should state any assumptions that you make.

Geometry and Measures
Strand 3 Measuring shapes
Unit 3 Circumference

PS PRACTISING SKILLS   **DF** DEVELOPING FLUENCY   **PB** PROBLEM SOLVING   **ES** EXAM-STYLE

PS **1** Find the circumference of these circles with radius

    a 4 cm

    b 7.5 m

    c 0.5 km.

Write your answers correct to two decimal places.

> Don't forget
> $C = \pi D$
> or
> $C = 2\pi r$

PS **2** Find the circumference of these circles with diameter

    a 6 cm

    b 3.5 m

    c 0.25 km.

    Write your answers correct to one decimal place.

PS **3** **a** A circle has a circumference of 78.5 cm. Find the diameter of the circle. Give your answer correct to 1 decimal place.

    b A circle has a circumference of 1 m. Find the radius of the circle. Give your answer correct to 2 decimal places.

DF **ES** **4** Derek makes a semi-circular flower bed. The radius of the flower bed is 90 cm. Find the perimeter of the flower bed.

DF **ES** **5** Carlie makes a cake with a diameter of 25 cm. She puts a ribbon around the middle of the cake. Carlie allows an overlap of 2 cm for the ribbon.

How long is the ribbon? Give your answer to the nearest centimetre.

PB **ES** **6** Jamie makes jewellery. She makes a brooch from a semicircle and an equilateral triangle.

Find the perimeter of the brooch. Give your answer correct to 2 decimal places.

5 cm

PB **ES** **7** Naga is making a fish pond in her garden. The fish pond is in the shape of a quarter circle. The radius of the circle is 1.5 metres. Naga is planning to create a path around the pond.

Find the perimeter of the pond. Give your answer to the nearest cm.

1.5 m

PB **ES** **8** Sid is marking out a netball court in the school hall. The court is made up from three rectangles and two semicircles. Sid is using tape to mark out the lines. Each roll of tape contains 50 m of tape.

29 m
15 m
5 m
5 m

Here is a diagram that shows the lines on the court. Work out how many rolls of tape Sid needs to buy.

PB **ES** **9** Michael is making a stained glass window. He uses pieces of lead to hold the glass in place. The rectangular window is made from two semicircles and 6 straight edges.

Work out the total length of the lead to make the window. Give your answer to the nearest centimetre.

90 cm
180 cm

PB **ES** **10** Rose is making a flower bed. The flower bed is made from two semicircles. The radius of the large semicircle is 3 m. The radius of the small semicircle is 1 m.

Rose is going to put lengths of edging strip along each edge of the flower bed. The edging strip is sold in lengths of 1.8 m.

How many edging strips will Rose need to buy?

3 m   1 m

Geometry and Measures
Strand 3 Measuring shapes
Unit 4 Area of circles

PS — PRACTISING SKILLS   **DF** — DEVELOPING FLUENCY   **PB** — PROBLEM SOLVING   **ES** — EXAM-STYLE

PS **1** Find the area of these circles with radius

    a 5 cm

    b 7 m

    c 3.2 cm.

    Give your answers correct to one decimal place.

Don't forget
Area $= \pi \times r^2$

PS **2** Find the area of these circles with diameter

    a 6 cm

    b 5 m

    c 0.8 km.

    Give your answers correct to one decimal place.

PS **3** **a** A circle has an area of 15.7 cm². Find the radius of the circle.
    Give your answer correct to two decimal places.

    b A circle has an area of 1 m². Find the diameter of the circle.
    Give your answer to the nearest centimetre.

DF **4** **a** A circle has an area of 50 cm². Find the circumference of the circle.
    Give your answer correct to one decimal place.

    b A circle has a circumference of 314 cm. Find the area of the circle.
    Give your answer correct to the nearest metre².

DF **ES** **5** Mo makes a semicircular flower bed. The radius
of the flower bed is 1.5 m.

Find the area of the flower bed. Give your answer
correct to 2 decimal places.

15 m

PB **ES** **6** Mia makes a semicircular carpet. The area of the carpet is 2.55 m².
Find the perimeter of the rug. Give your answer to the nearest cm.

PB **ES** **7** Naga feeds the fish in her fishpond. The fishpond is in the shape of a quarter circle. For every square metre of the area of the pond she gives the fish 25 g of fish food each day.

How many grams of fish food does she need to give the fish? Give your answer to the nearest gram.

2.5 m

PB **ES** **8** The diagram shows a circular pond surrounded by a path. The pond has a radius of 2.5 m. The path is 1 metre wide. The path is going to be covered with wood bark. Wood bark is sold in bags that cost £2.99 each. Each bag contains enough bark to cover 0.75 m².

Work out the cost of the wood bark needed to cover the path.

PB **ES** **9** Percy is making a lawn. The lawn is in the shape of half a ring made from two semicircles. The semicircles have the same centre. The radius of the large semicircle is 15 m. The radius of the small semicircle is 5 m.

Percy buys 1 kg boxes of lawn seed at £9 per box. Each kg of lawn seed covers 25 m². How much does it cost Percy to buy the grass seed?

15 m   5 m

DF **ES** **10** Paul makes a brooch. He makes it from a semicircle and two quarter circles of metal. The diameter of the semicircle is 4.5 cm. The radius of the large quarter circle is 2.5 cm. The radius of the small quarter circle is 1.5 cm.

Find the area of the brooch.

PB **ES** **11** This shape is made from a right-angled triangle, two semicircles and a quarter circle.

Find the area of this shape.

7.5 cm

6 cm

4.5 cm

Geometry and Measures
Strand 5 Transformations
Unit 6 Enlargement

PS · PRACTISING SKILLS   DF · DEVELOPING FLUENCY   PB · PROBLEM SOLVING   ES · EXAM-STYLE

PS 1 Here is a grid of squares.

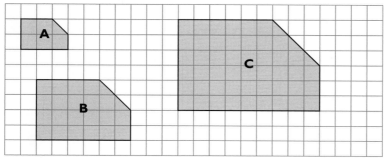

Write down the scale factor of the enlargement that takes
a A to B
b A to C
c B to C.

PS 2 Enlarge these shapes by scale factor 2. Use the cross marked nearest the shape as the centre of enlargement.

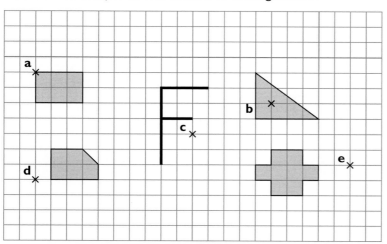

DF **3** Enlarge triangle P by

PB **a** scale factor 2 centre (−1, 0)

  b scale factor 3 centre (−4, 2).

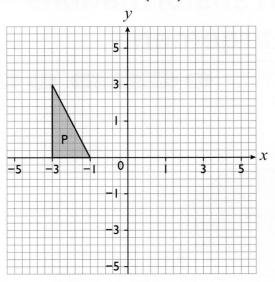

DF **4** Make three copies of this diagram. Enlarge triangle T by

PB **a** scale factor 3 centre (4, 3)

  b scale factor 2 centre (2, 2)

  c scale factor 1.5 centre (3, 1).

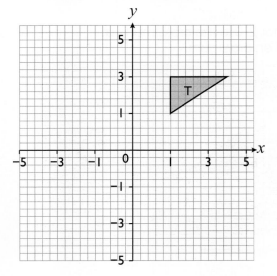

DF **5** Describe fully the single transformation that maps

    a triangle T onto triangle Q

    b triangle T onto triangle R.

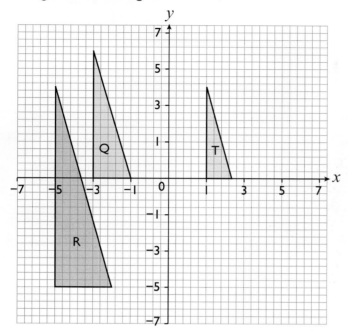

PB **6** Here is a small photograph. The small photograph is enlarged by scale factor 3 to make a large photograph.

ES What is the perimeter of the large photograph?

4 cm

←—6 cm—→

PB
ES

7 Here is a photograph. Jill makes enlargements of the photograph.

6 cm

8 cm

Enlargement A

32 cm

Enlargement B

16 cm

a Find the scale factor of the enlargement of Enlargement A.

b Find the width of Enlargement A.

c Work out the perimeter of Enlargement B.

PB
ES

8 Sophie has a picture she wants to put into a photograph frame. The photograph has a length of 5 cm and a width of 3 cm. The photograph frame has a length of 17.5 cm. She is going to enlarge the photograph to fit in the frame.

What width does the frame have to be to fit in the enlarged photograph?

3 cm

5 cm

17.5 cm

9 Enlarge triangle P by

    a scale factor $\frac{1}{2}$ centre $(-4, 4)$

    b scale factor $\frac{1}{3}$ centre $(-4, -5)$.

Geometry and Measures Strand 6 Three-dimensional shapes Unit 2 Understanding nets

PS — PRACTISING SKILLS   **DF** — DEVELOPING FLUENCY   **PB** — PROBLEM SOLVING   **ES** — EXAM-STYLE

PS
ES
1 Here is the net of a 3-D solid.
  a Write down the name of the solid.
  b Draw a 3-D sketch of the solid.

PS
ES
2 Here is a 3-D shape.
  a Write down the name of the shape.
  b Draw the net of the shape.

DF
3 Here is 3-D shape.
  a Write down the name of the shape.
  b Write down the number of
    i edges
    ii vertices
    iii faces.

PB
ES
4 Here is the net of a cube. There is a cross marked at one of the vertices. When the net is made into a cube which other corner meets the one marked with the cross?

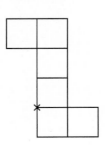

PB
ES **5** The diagram shows a box for chocolates.
The box is in the shape of a triangular prism.
Draw an accurate net for the box.

DF
ES **6** A box is in the shape of a cuboid with

length 5 cm
width 3 cm
height 2 cm.
Draw an accurate net of the cuboid.

PB
ES **7** A chocolate bar is in the shape of a triangular prism. A paper wrapper
covers the three rectangular faces of the chocolate bar. There is a 1 cm
additional flap on the wrapper.

Work out the length of the wrapper.

DF **8** A cube has 6 different faces.

Draw a net to show the faces in their position on the cube.

PB **9** Jim fixes a ribbon to the top corner P of a cuboid and the bottom
corner Q of the cuboid. PQR is a straight line.

Find, by drawing, the length of the ribbon PQR.

Geometry and Measures Strand 6 Three-dimensional shapes Unit 3 Volume and surface area of cuboids

PS — PRACTISING SKILLS   DF — DEVELOPING FLUENCY   PB — PROBLEM SOLVING   ES — EXAM-STYLE

PS **1** Work out the volume of these cuboids.

a 2 cm, 4 cm, 4 cm

b 3 cm, 12 cm, 8 cm

c 10 cm, 10 cm, 10 cm

PS **2** Work out the surface area of these cuboids.

a 2 cm, 3 cm, 5 cm

b 3 cm, 12 cm, 8 cm

c 10 cm, 10 cm, 10 cm

DF **3 a** A cube has a volume of 27 cm³. Find its surface area.

ES **b** A cube has a surface area of 96 cm². Find its volume.

PB **4** Here is diagram of a carton that contains one litre of orange juice.
ES The base of the container is a square of side 8 cm.
Find the least height of the container.

Orange Juice
I litre

1 litre = 1000 cm³

DF
ES

5 Phil has a box of toy bricks. Each toy brick is a cube with side 5 cm.
The box is full of toy bricks.

What is the greatest number of toy bricks that can fit into the box?

Toy bricks

10 cm
15 cm
30 cm

 DF
ES

6 Tea is sold in boxes. The boxes are 12 cm tall. The base is a square
of side 5 cm. The boxes of tea are delivered to shops in cartons. The
cartons are cuboids with length 60 cm, width 30 cm and height 36 cm.

Work out the greatest number of boxes of tea will fit into a carton.

T
E
A

12 cm
5 cm
5 cm

Carton

36 cm
30 cm
60 cm

PB
ES

7 An oil tank is in the shape of a cuboid.
The oil tank is 2.5 m by 1.5 m by 60 cm.

a Find the volume of the oil tank.

The oil tank is half full of oil.

b How much oil needs to be added to
the tank to fill it completely?

1 m³ = 1000 litres

PB
ES

8 Nick is going to paint his swimming pool. The pool stands on flat
ground and is in the shape of a cuboid. He is going to paint the four
outside faces and all the inside faces.

The pool has dimensions 15 m by 8 m by 1.2 m. The paint Nick is going
to use covers 15 m² with 1 litre of paint.
How many litres of paint will Nick need to buy?

PB

9 Jill designs a box with a lid. The box is to hold wooden discs which
have a radius of 6 cm and a height of 0.5 cm. Jill's box has to hold
up to 120 discs.

Work out the dimensions of a box that Jill could use.

PB
ES

10 Penny has a shed with a flat roof. The roof is a rectangle with length
1.8 m and width 1.2 m. One night 2.5 cm of rain fell on the roof and
was collected in a container that is in the shape of a cuboid.

The container has a height of 1.5 m and has a square base of
side 30 cm. At the beginning of the night there was 10 cm of rain
in the container.
Work out the height of the water in the container at the end of
the night.

Geometry and Measures Strand 6 Three-dimensional shapes Unit 4 2-D representations of 3-D shapes

 PS — PRACTISING SKILLS   DF — DEVELOPING FLUENCY   PB — PROBLEM SOLVING   ES — EXAM-STYLE

PB **1** Here is a 3-D drawing of Graham's garage. The front face and back face are rectangles. The other two vertical faces are trapeziums.

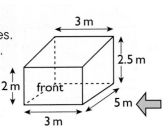

On squared paper, using a scale of 1 cm to represent 1 m

a draw a plan of the garage

b draw the front elevation of the garage

c draw the side elevation of the garage from the direction shown by the arrow.

DF **2** Here are some mathematical shapes. They have all got square bases of side 5 cm. On squared paper sketch for each shape

a the plan

b the front elevation

c the side elevation.

PS **3** Here are the plan, front elevation and side elevation of a 3-D shape.
ES Draw a sketch of the 3-D shape.

DF **ES** **4** Here are the plan, front elevation and side elevation of a shape that has been made from centimetre cubes.

Draw a sketch of the 3-D solid made from these cubes.
Use isometric paper.

Plan **Front elevation** **Side elevation**

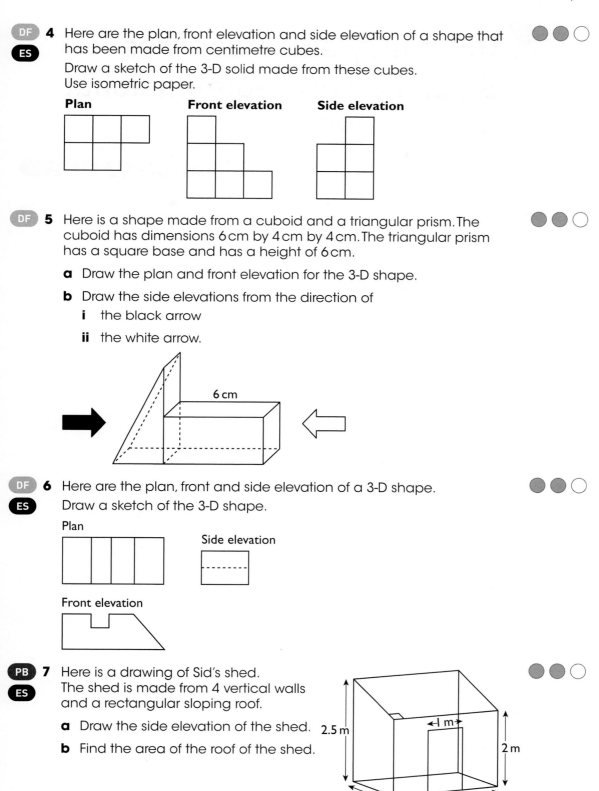

DF **5** Here is a shape made from a cuboid and a triangular prism. The cuboid has dimensions 6cm by 4cm by 4cm. The triangular prism has a square base and has a height of 6cm.

  a Draw the plan and front elevation for the 3-D shape.

  b Draw the side elevations from the direction of
    i the black arrow
    ii the white arrow.

6 cm

DF **ES** **6** Here are the plan, front and side elevation of a 3-D shape.
Draw a sketch of the 3-D shape.

Plan

Side elevation

Front elevation

PB **ES** **7** Here is a drawing of Sid's shed.
The shed is made from 4 vertical walls and a rectangular sloping roof.

  a Draw the side elevation of the shed.
  2.5 m
  b Find the area of the roof of the shed.

←1 m→

2 m

2 m

2 m

Geometry and Measures Strand 6 Three-dimensional shapes Unit 5 Prisms

PS — PRACTISING SKILLS   DF — DEVELOPING FLUENCY   PB — PROBLEM SOLVING   ES — EXAM-STYLE

PS 1 Here are some prisms. Find their volume.

a   20 cm²   5 cm

b   15 cm²   6 cm

c   12 cm²   4 cm

PS 2 Here are some prisms. Find their total surface area.

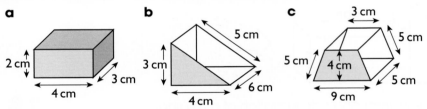

a   2 cm   3 cm   4 cm

b   5 cm   3 cm   4 cm   6 cm

c   3 cm   5 cm   5 cm   4 cm   5 cm   9 cm

PS 3 Here is a cylinder.
ES

   a Find the volume of the cylinder.

   b Find the total surface area of the cylinder.

   8 cm   3 cm

DF 4 Answer these.

   a A hexagonal prism has a cross-sectional area of 35 cm² and a length of 5 cm. Find the volume of the hexagonal prism.

   b A cylinder has a volume 1 litre. The area of the circular base is 50 cm². Find the height of the cylinder.

   c An octagonal prism has a volume of 24 cm³. The length of the prism is 3 cm. Find the area of the base of the prism.

102

PB
ES
5 Here is a sketch of Fred's shed. It is in the shape of a pentagonal prism. Fred is going to paint the 6 outside faces of the shed. 1 litre of the paint he uses covers 15 m².

How many litres of paint does he need?

DF
6 Siân makes a plant pot holder for her garden from a cylindrical block of wood. The cylinder has a diameter of 30 cm and a height of 30 cm. Siân cuts a hole with radius 10 cm to a depth of 20 cm into the cylinder.

What volume of wood is left from the original cylinder?

PB
ES
7 Susi is going to grow vegetables in a container in her garden. The container is in the shape of a prism. The ends of the prism are trapeziums.

Susi plans to fill the container completely with compost to a depth of 60 cm.
Compost is sold in 65 litre bags.
How many bags of compost will Susi need to buy?

| 1 m³ = 1000 litres |

PB
ES
8 Rhodri has a tank in his garden to store heating oil. The tank is in the shape of a square prism. The tank measures 60 cm by 1.2 m by 1.2 m. The level of oil in the tank is 30 cm from the bottom. Rhodri orders 700 litres of heating oil.

Will there be enough room in the oil tank for all the oil?
You must explain your answer.

PB
ES
9 A can of baked beans has a height of 10 cm and a radius of 3.7 cm. The average space needed for one baked bean is 0.2 cm³.
Estimate the number of baked beans in the tin.

PB
ES
10 Zigi has a swimming pool in the shape of a cylinder. The swimming pool has a diameter of 1.2 m. The height of the swimming pool is 90 cm. Zigi empties the swimming pool at a rate of 5 litres of water per minute. She starts emptying the pool at 8.30 a.m.

At what time will the swimming pool be completely empty?

Geometry and Measures Strand 6 Three-dimensional shapes Unit 6 Enlargement in two and three dimensions

PS PRACTISING SKILLS   **DF** DEVELOPING FLUENCY   **PB** PROBLEM SOLVING   **ES** EXAM-STYLE

PS **1** Here are two circles. One circle has a radius of 5 cm. The other circle has a diameter of 5 cm.

    a Find the ratio of the diameters.

    b Work out the ratio of their areas.

PS **2** A block of flats is in the shape of a cuboid. Nathan makes a scale model of the block of flats. He uses a scale of 1 cm to represent 50 cm.

    a The height of the block of flats is 30 m. What is the height of the model?

    b The area of the front of the model is 300 cm². What is the area of the front of the block of flats?

    c The model has dimensions 10 cm by 25 cm by 30 cm. Find the volume of the block of flats.

PB
ES **3** Mario has a small photograph that he is going to enlarge on his computer. The length of the small photograph and the length of the enlargement are in the ratio 2 : 5.

    a Find the perimeter of the enlargement.

    b Find the area of the enlargement.

4 cm

6 cm

DF **4** The grey box of matches is an enlargement of the black box of matches.

   a The height of the black box is 2 cm. What is the height of the grey box?

   b The area of the base of the grey box is 108 cm². What is the area of the base of the black box?

   c The volume of the black box is 24 cm³. What is the volume of the grey box?

   d Find the width, w, of the grey box of matches.

   e The black box of matches holds an average of 40 matches. How many matches will the grey box hold?

DF **5** This cuboid has a surface area of 484 cm².

   a Find the height of the cuboid.

   b Find the volume of the cuboid.

   The cuboid is enlarged by scale factor 5.

   c Find the surface area of this cuboid.

   d Find the volume of this cuboid.

PB
ES **6** The large watering can is an enlargement of the small watering can. The large can is twice the height of the small can. It takes Susan 30 seconds to fill the small watering can.

   How long will it take to fill the large watering can using the same tap?

PB **7**
ES

Lucy packs packets of tea into cartons.
The carton is an enlargement of the tea
packet. The ratio of the height of the tea
packet to the height of the carton is 1:4.

What is the most number of packets of tea
that will fit into the carton?

PB **8**
ES

Lesley is designing a banner to advertise a concert. He designs
this banner on his computer. The full size banner will fit across the
doorway of the venue. The doorway has a width of 3.75 m.
The banner costs £26 per square metre to make.

Work out the cost of the banner.

Concert
here Today

3 cm

7.5 cm

PB **9**
ES

Keith is making a model of a football stadium using a scale
of 1:1000. The area of the base of the stadium in Keith's model
is 2500 cm².

a Find the area of the base of the actual stadium.

The volume of the actual stadium is 10 000 000 m³.

b Find the volume of Keith's model.

Statistics and probability
Strand 1 Statistical measures
Unit 3 Using frequency tables

PS PRACTISING SKILLS   **DF** DEVELOPING FLUENCY   **PB** PROBLEM SOLVING   **ES** EXAM-STYLE

PS **1** Betty recorded the number of marks some students achieved in a test. Here are her results.

Number of marks	Frequency
7	4
8	14
9	8
10	6

  a How many students did the test?

  b Write down the mode.

  c Find the median.

  d Work out the mean.

PS **2** A taxi driver recorded the number of people he carried for each of 30 fares. Here are his results.

Number of people	Frequency
1	15
2	9
3	6

  a Write down the mode.

  b Find the median.

  c Work out the total number of people carried.

  d Work out the mean.

DF **3** Here are the numbers of eggs in each of 29 sparrow's nests.

2	3	5	5	3	5	2	4	5	4
3	4	4	2	4	3	5	5	4	4
4	3	5	4	4	3	3	2	5	

  a Construct a frequency table for this data.

  b Draw a bar chart for your frequency table.

  c Write down the mode.

  d Work out the mean. Give your answer correct to 2 decimal places.

DF **4** Hoeg sells shirts. The table gives information about the shirts he
sold on Friday and on Saturday.

Collar size	Frequency on Friday	Frequency on Saturday
14	4	0
$14\frac{1}{2}$	7	9
15	17	15
$15\frac{1}{2}$	32	28
16	30	37
$16\frac{1}{2}$	16	19

a On which day did Hoeg sell the most shirts?

b For each day
  i write down the mode
  ii find the range.

c Compare the modes and the ranges for these two days.

d Construct a frequency table for the data for Friday and
Saturday combined.

e Use your frequency table to find the median collar size for
the combined data.

DF
ES
5 The bar chart gives information about the numbers of letters Fritz
received on each of 25 days.

a Construct a frequency
table for this information.

b Work out the total
number of letters
Fritz got.

c Work out the mean
number of letters
each day.

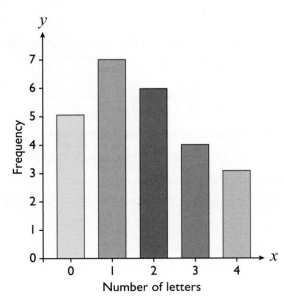

PB **ES** **6** 75 males and 75 females were asked to rate a film on a score of 1 to 5. A score of 5 represents the highest rating. Here are the results.

Male	
Score	Frequency
1	5
2	11
3	22
4	29
5	8

Female	
Score	Frequency
1	2
2	15
3	19
4	35
5	4

a Find the mode, median and mean for the males and for the females.

b Sam says: 'On average the males liked the film more than the females.' Is she right? Give a reason for your answer.

PB **ES** **7** The stem and leaf diagram shows information about the weights, in grams, of a sample of bats. The bats in the sample are all the same species.

2	4 6 9
3	0 1 2 4 4 4 4 7 8
4	3 5 6 6 7 9
5	2 4

Key: 2 | 4 represents 24 grams

a Write down the modal weight.

b Work out the range of the weights.

The mean weight of a bottle-nose bat is 40 grams.

c Do you think the bats in the sample are bottle-nosed bats? Explain your answer.

PB **ES** **8** Naveed records the numbers of books of stamps he sells. On Monday he sold:

  1 book of stamps to each of 8 people
  2 books of stamps to each of 14 people
  3 books of stamps to each of 23 people.
  Naveed also sold 4 books of stamps to a number of other people and kept a record. He can't read what he recorded. He knows he sold a total of 125 books of stamps on Monday.

Work out the number of people he sold 4 books of stamps to.

PB **9** Charles is the manager of a coffee shop. The table gives some information about the drinks he sold on Thursday.

Drink	Cost	Frequency
Coffee	£2.99	62
Tea	£1.99	49
Orange squash	£1.25	25
Orange juice	£2.49	12
Blackcurrant juice	£1.25	20

a Work out the range of the costs.

Charles makes a profit if the total amount he gets from drinks is greater than £200.

b Does Charles make a profit? How much profit?

c Work out the mean cost of a drink.

Charles thinks that he will sell more than 250 drinks on Friday.

d Find an estimate for the least amount of money he expects to earn on drinks sold on Friday.

Statistics and probability
Strand 1 Statistical measures
Unit 4 Using grouped frequency tables

PS — PRACTISING SKILLS   **DF** — DEVELOPING FLUENCY   **PB** — PROBLEM SOLVING   **ES** — EXAM-STYLE

PS
ES
1 The table shows information about the weights of 50 onions.

Weight (grams), w	Frequency, f	Midpoint, m	$f \times m$
$70 < w \leqslant 90$	12	80	960
$90 < w \leqslant 110$	23		
$110 < w \leqslant 130$	10		
$130 < w \leqslant 150$	5		

  a In which group does the median lie?

  b Copy and complete the table.

  c Find an estimate for the mean weight.

PS
ES
2 The number of complaints received by a TV company on each of 25 days is summarised in the table.

Number of complaints	Frequency, f	Midpoint, m	$f \times m$
0–2	3	1	3
3–5	11		
6–8	7		
9–11	4		

  a Copy and complete the table.

  b Find an estimate for the mean number of complaints.

  c Find an estimate for the range.

DF **3** In an experiment, some children were asked to do a jigsaw puzzle. The table shows information about the times taken to do the jigsaw puzzle.

Time (minutes), t	Frequency, f	Midpoint, m	$f \times m$
$5 < t \leqslant 7$	6		
$7 < t \leqslant 9$	18		
$9 < t \leqslant 11$	13		
$11 < t \leqslant 13$	8		
$13 < t \leqslant 15$	5		

a Write down the modal group.

b How many children did the jigsaw puzzle?

c In which group does the median lie?

d Copy and complete the table.

e Find an estimate for the mean time.

DF **4** In a land survey the areas of 90 fields are measured. The results are summarised in the table.

Area (hectares), a	Frequency, f
$0 < a \leqslant 10$	9
$10 < a \leqslant 20$	15
$20 < a \leqslant 30$	23
$30 < a \leqslant 40$	28
$40 < a \leqslant 50$	15

a Work out the number of fields with an area

   i greater than 30 hectares

   ii 40 hectares or less.

b Write down the modal group.

c Estimate the mean area of the fields.

PB **5** There are 100 trees in Ashdown Woods. The table gives information about the
ES   heights of 85 of these trees.

Height (metres), h	Frequency, f
$0 < h \leqslant 4$	30
$4 < h \leqslant 8$	24
$8 < h \leqslant 12$	15
$12 < h \leqslant 16$	12
$16 < h \leqslant 20$	4

Here are the heights, in metres, of the other 15 trees.

3.5	10.3	11.4	6.7	3.9
4.2	12.5	2.4	15.8	17.0
9.5	8.9	14.9	15.2	7.8

  a Draw and complete a frequency table for all 100 trees.

  b Write down the modal group.

  c Find an estimate for the mean height of the 100 trees.

PB **6** The manager of a shoe shop recorded the amounts of money
ES   spent on shoes in one day. Her results are summarised in the table.

Amount spent (£), a	Frequency, f
$0 < a \leqslant 25$	4
$25 < a \leqslant 50$	26
$50 < a \leqslant 75$	63
$75 < a \leqslant 100$	17

  a Work out an estimate for the total amount of money spent on
     shoes that day.

  b Find an estimate for the mean.

  c Explain why this is only an estimate of the mean.

PB **7** Mrs Abdul takes some children to a theme park. The tables
ES   give information about the heights of the children.

Boys	
Height (cm), h	Frequency, f
$120 < h \leqslant 125$	0
$125 < h \leqslant 130$	3
$130 < h \leqslant 135$	7
$135 < h \leqslant 140$	16
$140 < h \leqslant 145$	9

Girls	
Height (cm), h	Frequency, f
$120 < h \leqslant 125$	1
$125 < h \leqslant 130$	3
$130 < h \leqslant 135$	8
$135 < h \leqslant 140$	15
$140 < h \leqslant 145$	8

a Compare the mean heights of the boys and girls.

One of the rides at the theme park has a height restriction.
Children with a height of 130 cm or less cannot go on the ride.

b What percentage of the children cannot go on the ride?

PB **ES** **8** The incomplete table below shows some information about the body temperatures of the patients in a hospital.

Temperature (°C), T	Frequency, f	Midpoint, m	$f \times T$
$36.25 < T \leqslant 36.75$	15	36.5	
$36.75 < T \leqslant 37.25$	19		703
$37.25 < T \leqslant 37.75$		37.5	450
	10	38	380
$38.25 < T \leqslant 38.75$	4		

a Copy and complete the table.

b Find an estimate for the mean body temperature of the patients.

c In which group does the median lie?

A patient has a fever if they have a body temperature greater than 38°C.

d Find the best estimate for the number of patients with a fever.

PB **ES** **9** Balpreet recorded the lifetimes in hours, h, of some batteries. Here are her results.

11.0	10.5	14.2	16.3	18.3	14.8	15.8	12.5	17.9	13.9
15.5	16.3	15.4	17.7	12.3	19.5	13.6	16.8	14.3	14.9
14.5	12.8	13.6	17.6	15.0	14.2	19.6	15.7	13.1	15.7

a Work out the mean lifetime of the batteries.

b Draw and complete a grouped frequency table for this data using the intervals $10 < h \leqslant 12, 12 < h \leqslant 14$, etc.

c Use your grouped frequency table to calculate an estimate for the mean lifetime of the batteries.

d Is your estimate an overestimate or an underestimate of the mean lifetime of the batteries? Explain why.

Statistics and probability
Strand 2 Statistical diagrams
Unit 3 Vertical line charts

PS — PRACTISING SKILLS   DF — DEVELOPING FLUENCY   PB — PROBLEM SOLVING   ES — EXAM-STYLE

PS 1 The vertical line chart shows the number of tropical fish that each of 5 students has.

   a Which student has the smallest number of fish?

   b Two of these students have the same number of fish. Which two students?

   c Tez has more fish than Ann. How many more?

   d Work out the total number of fish the 5 students have.

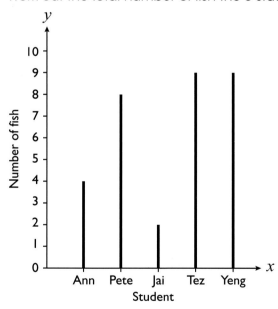

PS **2** Sethina sells donkey rides on the beach. The table shows the number of rides she sold in one week in June.

Day	Mon	Tue	Wed	Thu	Fri	Sat	Sun
Number of rides	15	20	15	25	25	45	40

a Draw a vertical line chart to show this information.

b Write down the mode.

c Sethina sold more rides at the weekend. Suggest a reason why.
Sethina charged £1.50 for each ride.

d Work out how much money she got that week.

DF **3** Sherry recorded the number of games won by 4 hockey teams, A, B, C and D. She drew this vertical line chart for her results.

Comment on any errors or omissions in Sherry's vertical line chart.

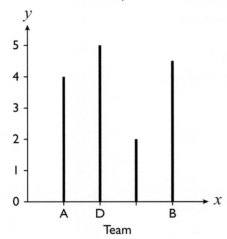

DF **4** A doctor recorded the blood groups of each of 30 patients.
Here are the results.

O	B	O	AB	O	A	A	O	A	O
A	O	A	O	AB	O	A	O	A	B
B	O	A	A	A	O	O	A	O	A

a Copy and complete the frequency table for this data.

Blood group	Tally	Frequency
O		
A		
B		
AB		

b Draw a vertical line chart for the information in your table.

c Write down the modal blood group.

d What percentage of these patients are blood group A?

PB **ES** **5** A stockbroker made 5 trade deals. The vertical line chart shows information about the amount of money gained or lost in each trade deal.

    a How much money was gained in trade deal 1?

    b How much money was gained in trade deal 3?

    c Work out the total amount of money gained for all 5 trade deals combined.

    d Work out the average amount of money gained per trade deal.

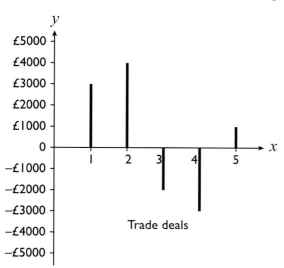

PB **ES** **6** John recorded the increase in height of 6 tomato plants in a week. Here are his results.

Plant	A	B	C	D	E	F
Increase in height (cm)	3	7	9	4	7	5

    a Draw a vertical line chart to show this information.

    b Which tomato plant had the greatest increase in height?

    Here are the heights of the tomato plants at the beginning of the week.

Plant	A	B	C	D	E	F
Height at beginning of week (cm)	45	46	39	47	49	40

    c Which tomato plant had the greatest height at the end of the week?

    d Compare the ranges of the heights of the tomato plants at the beginning of the week and at the end of the week.

PB
ES
7 The vertical line chart gives information about the numbers of
goals scored by a football team in each game of a competition.

   a Write down the modal number of goals scored.

   b How many games did the team play?

   c Work out the total number of goals scored by the team.

   d Work out the mean number of goals scored per game.

PB **8** The vertical line chart shows information about the numbers and
types of butterflies Sally saw in a garden in July and in August.

   a How many Marbled Whites were seen in July?

   b More Red Admirals were seen in July then in August.
How many more?

   c Work out the total number of Tortoiseshell butterflies seen in
July and August.

   d Sally says: 'I saw more butterflies in July than in August.'
Is she right? Show how you got your answer.

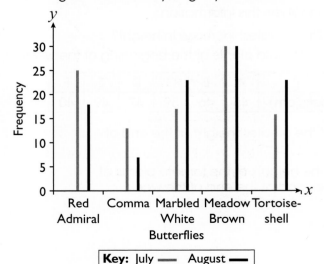

Key: July ── August ──

Statistics and probability
Strand 2 Statistical diagrams
Unit 4 Pie charts

PS — **PRACTISING SKILLS**   **DF** — **DEVELOPING FLUENCY**   **PB** — **PROBLEM SOLVING**   **ES** — **EXAM-STYLE**

PS **1** The pie chart shows information about the weights of the ingredients used to make a cake.

    a Which ingredient has

       i the smallest weight

       ii the largest weight?

    b What fraction of the cake is flour?
       Tony makes this cake. He uses
       125 grams of eggs.

    c Work out the total weight of the cake.

● ○ ○

PS **2** The pie chart shows information about the finances of a supermarket.

    a What fraction of the finances is profit?
       The angle for taxes is 90°.

    b Work out the angle used for costs.
       The taxes paid were £5000.

    c Work out

       i the profit made by the supermarket

      ii the supermarket's costs.

● ○ ○

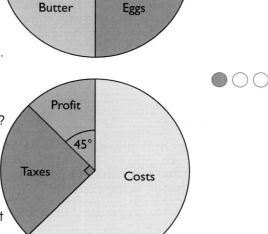

DF **3** The table gives the numbers of votes that Simon, Helga and Bik got in an election.

● ○ ○

	Simon	Helga	Bik
Number of votes	15	6	9

    Tania is going to draw a pie chart to show this information.

    a How many degrees should she use for one vote?

    b Work out the angle she should use for

       i Helga

      ii Simon.

c Tania says: 'Bik got more than a quarter of the votes.' Is she right?
Give a reason for your answer.

DF **4** The vertical line chart shows information about the counters in a bag. ●○○
A pie chart is to be drawn for this information.

    a How many degrees should be used for each counter?

    b Draw the pie chart.

    c What percentage of the counters are white?

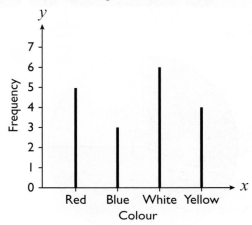

DF **5** Sophie takes photos on her mobile phone. The table shows information ●○○
about the numbers and types of photos she took in June.

Type of photo	Family	Holiday	Pets	Friends	Other
Frequency	36	78	60	87	9

Draw a pie chart to show this information.

PB
ES **6** Cleg recorded the numbers and types of trees in a park. His results ●○○
are summarised in the pie chart.

    a Measure the angle used for birch.

    b There are 240 trees in the park. Work out the number of birch trees
in the park.

    c There are more sycamore trees than oak trees. How many more?

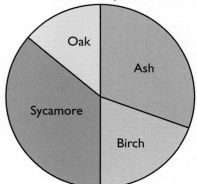

PB 7 In a survey, Phil asked some people what type of music they like the best.
ES They could choose from pop, jazz and classical. The pie charts give information about his results.

Phil asked the same number of females and males.

a Use the pie charts to compare the results for the females and the males. Write down two comparisons.

Phil asked a total of 68 females.

b Work out the number of males who like jazz the best.

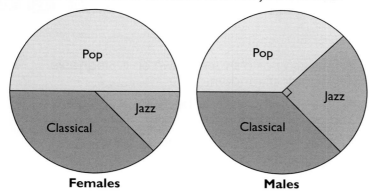

Females **Males**

PB 8 Sylus recorded the medals won by Great Britain in a competition.
ES Here are his results.

Gold	Silver	Bronze	Gold	Silver
Bronze	Bronze	Bronze	Bronze	Bronze
Bronze	Silver	Bronze	Silver	Bronze

Draw a pie chart for this information.

PB 9 Some students did a test. The incomplete table and pie chart
ES give some information about the grades awarded in the test.

Grade	E	D	C	B	A
Frequency			10	16	12
Angle used in pie chart	30				90

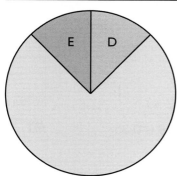

Copy and complete the table and pie chart. Use your table to complete the pie chart.

Statistics and probability
Strand 4 Probability Unit 2
Single event probability

PS 1 Here are some cards. Each card has a shape drawn on it. Stephanie is going to take one of the cards at random.

    a Which shape has the greater probability of being taken, an arrow or a heart? Give a reason for your answer.

    b Write down the probability that the shape will be an arrow.

PS 2 Jasmine rolls a biased die. The probability that the die will land on a 6 is 0.4.

Work out the probability that the die will not land on a 6.

PS 3 There are 3 red counters, 2 green counters and 6 yellow counters in a bag. Yuan is going to take, at random, a counter from the bag.

    a What is the probability that the counter will be

      i red

      ii green

      iii yellow

      iv white?

    b What is the probability the counter will **not** be

      i red

      ii green

      iii yellow

      iv white?

DF 4 The probability of event A is $\frac{1}{3}$. The probability of event B is 0.35.

The probability of event C is 30%.

Write these events in order of likelihood. Start with the least likely event.

DF 5 The vertical line chart shows the flavours and numbers of sweets in a box. Maja is going to take, at random, a sweet from the box.

a Which flavour of sweet has the smallest probability of being taken?

b Write down the probability that the flavour will be
  i strawberry
  ii lime.

c Write down the probability that the flavour will not be
  i orange
  ii lemon.

DF 6 The pie chart gives information about the ages of the people watching a film at a cinema.

One of these people is picked at random. Find the probability that the age of this person will be

a 51 years and over

b 50 years or less

c 31–50 years

d 11–30 years.

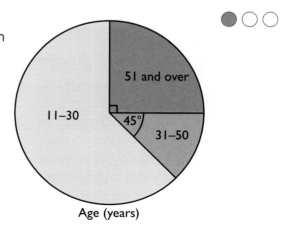

DF **7** The stem and leaf diagram gives the number of people on each of 25 tours.

1	7 7 8 9 9 9
2	1 2 3 3 3 4 4 6 6 6 8 9 9
3	0 0 1 2 2 3

Key: 1|7 represents 17 people

Henry picks, at random, one of these tours. What is the probability that this tour has on it

a exactly 26 people

b 19 people or less

c more than 25 people

d between 20 and 25 people?

PB **8** Katie is designing a fair spinner to use in her probability lessons. She is going to spin the spinner once.

Copy and complete the spinner for each question. You must only use letters A, B and C. Write 4 letters on the spinner so that it is

a more likely to get an A than a B

b equally likely to get an A or a C

c twice as likely to get a B than an A.

PB
ES **9** Box A contains 3 bags of ready salted crisps and 4 bags of cheese and onion crisps. Box B contains 4 bags of ready salted crisps and 7 bags of cheese and onion crisps.

Tiny is going to take, at random, a bag of crisps from one of the boxes. She wants to have the best chance of taking a bag of ready salted crisps.
Which box should she use? Explain why.

PB
ES **10** Silvia is designing a probability experiment. She puts 15 green counters and 35 blue counters in a bag.

a What is probability of taking, at random, a green counter from the bag?

Silvia puts some more blue counters in the bag. The probability of taking at random a green counter from the bag is now 0.25.

b How many blue counters did she put in the bag?

Statistics and probability
Strand 4 Probability Unit 3
Combined events

PS — PRACTISING SKILLS   DF — DEVELOPING FLUENCY   PB — PROBLEM SOLVING   ES — EXAM-STYLE

PS 1 Nathalie spins three fair coins. Here are the possible outcomes.

Write down the probability that she will get

a 3 heads

b one head and two tails

c two heads and a tail

d at least two heads.

PS 2 Simon goes to a restaurant. He can choose from three types of soup and from three types of bread.

Soup	Bread
Tomato	Brown
Vegetable	White
Lentil	Granary

Simon is going to choose one type of soup and one type of bread.

a List all the possible combinations Simon can choose.

Simon chooses, at random, one type of bread.

b Write down the probability that he will choose Granary.

PS **3** Here are some letters and some numbers on cards.

| A | B | C | 2 | 3 | 4 | 5 |

Safta is going to take, at random, one of the cards with a letter on it and one of the cards with a number on it.

a One possible combination is (A, 2). Write down all the other possible combinations.

b Write down the probability he will take

   i (A, 2)

   ii B and any number

   iii C and a prime number

   iv A or C and an even number.

DF **4** Wilhelm spins a fair 5-sided spinner and a fair 4-sided spinner.

	1	2	3	4
1	2	3	4	5
2	3	4		
3	4			
4				
5				

a Copy and complete the table to show all the possible total scores.

b What is the probability that the total score is

   i exactly 9

   ii exactly 7

   iii an odd number

   iv 4 or less.

DF **5** There are 50 students in a college. Each student may study Polish, Welsh and Chinese.

The Venn diagram gives information about the numbers of students studying all, two, one, or none of these languages.
One of the 50 students is picked at random.

a What is the probability that this student studies

   i all three languages

   ii only Polish

   iii both Chinese and Welsh

   iv Chinese?

One of the 17 students studying Welsh is picked at random.

b What is the probability that this student also studies

i Chinese

ii both Chinese and Polish?

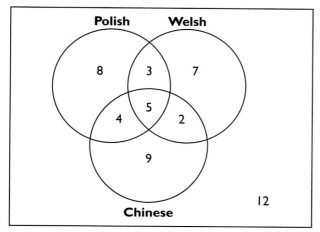

PB **6** Hoeg asked 59 people at a youth club if they play tennis or squash.
ES 35 people said they play tennis. 28 people said they play squash.
17 people said they play both tennis and squash.

a Copy and complete the Venn diagram.

One of these people is picked at random.

b Find the probability that this person plays

i squash

ii tennis, but not squash

iii tennis or squash, but not both

iv neither tennis nor squash.

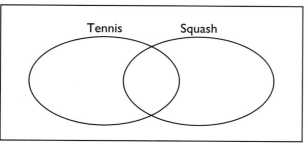

PB **7** Oparbi asked some children which of three films they like the best. ●○○
The incomplete table shows some information about her results.

	Minions	Inside out	Wall·E	Total
Boys	14	A	8	B
Girls	C	5	D	21
Total	20	E	F	47

a Find the missing values A–F.

One of these children is picked at random.

b What is the probability that this child will be

i a boy

ii a girl who likes *Minions* the best.

One of the girls is picked at random.

c What is the probability that this girl likes *Wall·E* the best?

PB **8** 130 students were each asked to choose an activity for a school trip. ●○○
ES The table gives information about these students and the activity they chose.

	Cinema	Theatre	Concert
Male	28	17	14
Female	32	23	16

One of the students is picked at random.

a Find the probability that this student

i is male

ii is a female who chose concert

iii is a male who did not choose cinema.

One of the male students is picked at random.

b Find the probability that this student

i chose theatre

ii did not choose concert.

PB **9** Here are some cards. Each card has a letter on it. Helen takes, at
random, two of the cards.

a Write down all the possible combinations. ●○○

b What is the probability that one of these two cards has S on it? ●○○

Jim takes, at random, three of the cards.

c Write down all the possible combinations. ●●○

d What is the probability that one of these three cards has S on it? ●●○

C	A	R	D	S